BETWEEN PARENT AND TEACHER

By

FRANCES CLAYTON WELCH, Ph.D.

Associate Professor
Department of Education
The College of Charleston
Charleston, South Carolina

and

PAMELA COCHRANE TISDALE, Ph.D.

Associate Professor
Department of Education
The College of Charleston
Charleston, South Carolina

CHARLES C THOMAS • PUBLISHER
Springfield • Illinois • U.S.A.

Published and Distributed Throughout the World by

CHARLES C THOMAS • PUBLISHER
2600 South First Street
Springfield, Illinois 62708-4709

© *1986 by* CHARLES C THOMAS • PUBLISHER

ISBN 0-398-05249-2

Library of Congress Catalog Card Number: 86-5724

Printed in the United States of America
Q-R-3

Library of Congress Cataloging in Publication Data

Welch, Frances Clayton.
    Between parent and teacher.

    Includes index.
    1. Parent-teacher   relationships.   2. School
children — Discipline.   3. Home   and   school.
4. Exceptional children — Education. I. Tisdale, Pamela
Cochrane.
II. Title.
LC225.W39   1986   371.1'03   86-5724
ISBN 0-398-05249-2

With respect and appreciation
this book is dedicated to our mothers

Dorothy Shuler Clayton
and
Helene Vortigern Cochrane

PREFACE

IT IS IMPORTANT for parents and teachers to understand each other's roles, responsibilities, problems and concerns in order to work together to maximize learning experiences of children. Unfortunately, parents sometimes feel intimidated by teachers and teachers feel threatened by parents. These feelings usually result from a lack of understanding and communication rather than because of lack of concern about the child's education.

In order to provide information, suggestions, and guidelines for parents and teachers about how to better work together, the authors began writing a column for a local newspaper entitled, "Between Parent and Teacher." This column was welcomed by parents and teachers, who requested copies of the articles as well as made suggestions for topics to be discussed in the column. Because the articles seemed beneficial to both parents and teachers in their attempts to work as a team, the authors decided to compile the articles from this column into a book. **Between Parent and Teacher** is designed to be a practical guide for parents and teachers as they plan, coordinate, communicate, and implement changes in an effort to improve the education of children. The authors encourage readers of the book to copy articles and activities and share them whenever this would be beneficial to parent-teacher cooperative efforts.

When the authors were organizing the articles into a manuscript for the book, five logical chapters emerged. The first chapter, "Communication and Cooperation," contains articles which address the essential elements for effective coordination between parents and teachers. The articles in this chapter provide suggestions for beginning and maintaining the communication process, planning for and having meaningful and productive conferences, realizing the importance of teacher morale and expectations, and effectively communicating with children.

An area which results in great concern and discussion for parents and teachers is discipline and management. The articles in Chapter 2, "Discipline: A Cooperative Venture," provide practical and applied suggestions for parents and teachers in order to complement each other's approaches for the management of children. One very important aspect of these articles is that they give parents and teachers a common vocabulary and set of procedures which are understood. Thus, when parents and teachers are attempting to effectively manage children's behavior they have a common ground from which to work. In the articles in this chapter, suggestions are provided for contracting, time out, and token ecomonies, and the importance of being consistent and positive is emphasized.

There are many activities in schools that are routine in nature. It is beneficial when both parents and teachers are aware of their specific responsibilities in these regularly occurring activities so that cooperation rather than misunderstanding results. Chapter 3, "The School Routine," includes articles which provide information about school routines and ways teachers and parents can work together to make these quality experiences for children and adults.

The most important time for parents and teachers to work as a team is when a specific problem has been identified. Information about possible problems and suggestions for teachers, parents, and other professionals to use when they encounter these are given in Chapter 4, "Special Children and Problems."

After the authors completed the organization of the first four chapters, there remained a number of articles that did not fit any specific category but were considered of importance for parent-teacher cooperation. These articles deal with topics such as computers in education, nutrition, time management, and summer vacation. They are included in Chapter 5, "Other Topics of Mutual Concern."

Although the authors have a commitment to nonsexist language, they in most cases referred to the teacher as "she" in the book. The decision to do this was consciously made because it is less cumbersome and wordy, and it is true that in 1986 most teachers are females.

The authors hope that readers will find **Between Parent and Teacher** to be as useful and practical as it was intended to be. The authors have attempted to be as brief and straightforward as possible and to use vocabulary which is understood by both parents and teachers. The Table of Contents and Subject Index are organized so that topics of concern can be easily located.

The wish of the authors as they complete this manuscript is that teachers and parents will be able to work together meaningfully, enjoyably, and effectively so that the educational experiences of children will be more meaningful, enjoyable, and effective. The authors hope that teachers, parents and other educational professionals use their book to make this wish a reality.

CONTENTS

Page

Preface vii

Chapter I: COMMUNICATION AND COOPERATION 3
   Introduction 3
   Establishing lines of communication 5
   Promoting teacher-parent cooperation 8
   Planning for a conference 12
   The problem solving conference........................... 14
   Teacher morale: What teachers and parents can do........... 16
   The importance of expectations 20
   Effective communication with children 22
Chapter II: DISCIPLINE: A COOPERATIVE VENTURE 25
   Introduction 25
   What is behavior modification? 27
   The "SPI" approach to discipline 29
   Using rewards effectively................................. 31
   Contingency contracting or "Grandma's Law" 34
   The home-school contract 35
   Token economies in home and school 38
   How to use response cost as punishment.................... 41
   Using "time out" at home and school 43
   Corporal punishment: Reasons not to use it................ 45
   Are you caught in the "Criticism Trap"? 51
   Your "Discipline Quotient" 54
Chapter III: THE SCHOOL ROUTINE 63
   Introduction 63
   Homework from the teacher's perspective.................. 65

Page

Homework from the parent's perspective 67
Grading and reporting progress 68
Parents as volunteers 69
When a child needs tutoring 71
The hidden curriculum 72
Teachable moments 73
Chapter IV: SPECIAL CHILDREN AND PROBLEMS 75
Introduction 75
What is special education? 76
Utilizing special personnel in schools..................... 78
Children and stress...................................... 81
Identifying learning disabilities 85
Understanding and managing children with attention
  deficit disorder...................................... 86
School phobia: When a child avoids school................. 89
The gifted and talented: A challenge for parents
  and teachers... 91
Chapter V: OTHER TOPICS OF MUTUAL CONCERN 93
Introduction 93
The link between nutrition and behavior 95
Time management: When you have too much to do
  and too little time 97
Computers in education: The present, the possibilities,
  the problems 99
The importance of recognizing a child's learning style 102
The bifunctional brain in the classroom 104
A productive summer vacation..........................106

Index 109

BETWEEN PARENT
AND
TEACHER

CHAPTER 1

COMMUNICATION AND COOPERATION

INTRODUCTION

THE PRIMARY elements for effective working relationships between teachers and parents are communication and cooperation. When teachers and parents are able to cooperate and communicate openly and honestly about the education of children, better programs result. The first step in this process is to establish lines of communication. The first article in this chapter, "Establishing Lines of Communication," provides suggestions for beginning the communication process and establishing an effective working relationship. The second step is to promote teacher-parent cooperation, and the second article, "Promoting Teacher-Parent Cooperation," includes guidelines to follow in order to accomplish this.

Parent-teacher conferences are an important aspect of cooperation and communication. The next two articles provide recommendations for effective conferencing. The first "Planning for a Conference," suggests guidelines to follow when planning for a conference and the second, "The Problem-Solving Conference," provides suggestions when a child's problems could best be solved by a cooperative effort.

Knowing about and understanding teacher morale is another important component of effective parent-teacher cooperation. Both

3

parents and teachers should be aware of teacher morale and activities which can be implemented to improve it. Improved teacher moral results in improved educational programs for children, and this is discussed in "Teacher Morale: What Teachers and Parents Can Do."

In addition to cooperating and communicating with each other, parents and teachers will be more effective when they are able to establish appropriate expectations for children and this is discussed in "The Importance of Expectations." Adults should also promote productive communication with children. "Effective Communication with Children" provides suggestions for parents and teachers when they are attempting to communicate effectively.

ESTABLISHING LINES OF COMMUNICATION

Cooperation between parents and teachers is often the key to maximizing children's educational experiences. This cooperation enables parents and teachers to work as a team, the goals of which are to enable children to obtain the greatest possible benefit from their education, and to enable them to realize their potential.

To make this cooperative effort possible, lines of communication must be established between parents and teachers. Establishment of these lines of communication helps ensure that the parents and teachers become aware of each others feelings, thoughts, and expectations.

Unfortunately, parents and teachers usually wait until a problem arises before a contact is made. This decreases the possibility of effective communication and cooperation. Communication should be established as soon after the beginning of the school year as possible. It does not matter whether the teacher or the parent initiates the first contact. What matters is that the contact is made.

One possible outcome of this contact is an informal meeting held in the child's classroom. At this initial meeting, the teacher should make the parents feel welcome, realizing that many parents do not feel comfortable in the school environment.

There are several ways teachers may help parents feel more comfortable in the classroom and school setting. The first is obvious but sometimes difficult to remember after a long day in school: It is to greet parents cheerfully; a smile is worth 1,000 words! A teacher's smile lets the parents know that the teacher is happy to see them and pleased that they have come. A second suggestion for the teacher is to sit next to, and on the same level, as parents. Sometimes a teacher will ask parents to sit in a student's desk while she sits behind her desk. This arrangement of furniture establishes a barrier between the parents and teacher. If the parents must sit in a student's desk then the teacher should also.

The teacher should explain and review the rules, goals and procedures for the school and her classroom using language that the parents can understand. Parents should be encouraged to sit in their child's desk, inspect their child's textbooks, and become familiar with the daily classroom routine.

The teacher should inform the parents of procedures for scheduling future conferences. Sharing details such as whether to call the teacher at home or at school, and when, will be helpful to both the teacher and parents. If a routine home-school communication system will be used (such as papers home every Friday to be returned with the parent's signature on Monday), this should be discussed.

Parents should discuss their own goals for their child as well as what they expect from the school environment. Any special needs of the child, such as medication, diet, learning style, and interests, should be explained. Parents should specify how and when the teacher could contact them when necessary. Questions should be asked about any classroom or home-school procedure that is not fully understood.

It is the responsibility of both parents and teachers to set the stage for a productive school year by establishing lines of communication. Even though it is best to do this at the beginning of the school year, it is never too late. Communication will enable parents and teachers to work as team members to create successful learning experiences for their children.

The list of guidelines which follows should be helpful to both parents and teachers when attempting to establish lines of communication.

Guidelines for Initial Conferences Between Parents and Teachers

_____ Learn names.
           Teacher's name: _____
           Parent's name: _____

_____ Conference early in the school year before there is a problem.

_____ Smile and be as relaxed and comfortable as possible.

_____ Begin and end with positive comments.

_____ Use appropriate vocabulary which is mutually understood.

_____ Communicate goals for child and other significant information such as health problems, diet restrictions, school rules and procedures.

_____ Learn how to make contact for follow-up conferences.

Where to call: _____

When to call: _____

Telephone #: _____

Notes:

PROMOTING TEACHER-PARENT COOPERATION

Teachers should establish good relationships with parents if they want to make significant educational progress with children. Likewise, parents should establish good relationships with teachers if they want their children to obtain maximum benefit from educational experiences. This is logical and most agree that a cooperative relationship will have positive effects on children. If research evidence is needed to verify the importance of a cooperative arrangement between parents and teachers, there are numerous studies which show that when parents and teachers work together, the children are the winners: achievement scores rise, self-concepts improve, and grades are better.

It is easy to say that cooperation is necessary, it is the doing it that is difficult. What can parents and teachers do to promote a cooperative working arrangement? A number of suggestions to guide parents and teachers as they work together will be presented. These guidelines come from a variety of sources: the educational literature, teachers, parents, and our experience while working with parents, teachers, and children.

1. Make Every Child a Winner.

What is meant by, "every child a winner"? Is being a winner the same thing as winning? No! ! ! The winner is a child who achieves to his or her maximum potential without comparison to others and can make positive statements about him or herself. The child who is a winner recognizes his or her strengths and weaknesses and tries to improve weaknesses while giving positive self-feedback about strengths. The real winner feels good when others win. The winner may not be the child who makes all A's, wins the beauty contest or the spelling bee, or is the best athlete; but everybody can be a winner while only one can win.

2. Work to Build a Positive Self-Concept.

Whose self-concept? The child's, of course, but also that of the parents and teacher. The adults in the cooperative working arrangement should feel good about themselves and understand who they are and what they are trying to accomplish. It is difficult to work cooperatively with someone else until you believe that you are competent and capable. Teachers and parents must like and respect themselves, feel competent and responsible, be self-assured, and not threatened by others. Having a realistic self-concept means not being overly self-assured nor underestimating abilities. In order to work cooperatively, parents and teachers must "get their acts together" as individuals, know what they believe, feel unique, and in control of their lives. In short, the parents and teachers must see themselves as winners. This means that neither the parents nor the teacher should be living their lives through those of the children.

3. Make a Time Commitment.

If parents and teachers want to work together, they must be willing to make and take the time to do so. Since good communication and cooperative working arrangements take time, many problems are created by a lack of communication. One way to create time for communication is to use the time spent complaining about a problem to try and solve it.

4. Remember That the Teacher is the Professional.

The educational team is composed of the child's teacher(s), and parent(s), and sometimes other school personnel (nurse, principal, counselor, social worker, etc.). The teacher is the captain of this team and is in charge of the education of the children in her class. Because the teacher has received specialized training which enables her to plan for and instruct the child, she is a professional. Thus, the parent(s) should view and treat the teacher as a professional who is competent to do her job. In treating the teacher as a professional, parents should arrange mutually suitable times for conferences and give the teacher as the professional the freedom to conduct educational activities as she deems appropriate. As a professional, the teacher should engage in activities which will warrant the parent's respect. Also, she should respect the parents, solicit their input and provide them with feedback about their child's performance.

5. Don't Pass the Buck.

Both parents and teachers have a tendency to think of excuses for the child's inappropriate behaviors or problems. They often "pass the buck" and say that the problem is the fault of the last teacher, the former school, hyperactivity, the child's being just like his father or mother, the divorce, a learning problem, or illness. Parents and teachers should try to avoid spending large amounts of time in this way. They must be open, trustful, and frank with each other, refrain from talking in generalities, and specifically and nondefensively discuss the exact behaviors that are occurring. After stating the problem behaviors, the parents and teachers can begin making plans for an appropriate intervention to change the particular behaviors.

6. Stay in Control.

Whenever teachers and parents meet, all parties should try to remain calm, patient, and objective. Sometimes when meetings between teachers and parents are held to discuss difficult or controversial subjects, both the teachers and parents can be very emotionally involved. Often in these situations, parents and teachers will make statements that are hurtful and create anger for the other. When either the parents or the teacher makes such statements, the other should remember that becoming angry will do little to solve the problem. If one party is particularly distraught and has a prepared discourse to render, the other party should attempt to listen intelligently, reflect what has been said, and then present informaiton as factually as possible. Remember that the best decisions are made with the intellect rather than the emotions and that it takes at least two persons to argue.

7. Support Each Other.

The parents and teacher should let the child know that they support each other and have mutually acceptable information and plans. This type of teamwork can assist the child in overcoming problems. Use of the word "we" can convey to the child this mutual support and agreement, i.e., "We have agreed to have a home-school contract in an effort to help you."

After communication has been established, parents and teachers can promote a cooperative working relashionship by following the seven suggestions which have been discussed. These are:

1. Make every child a winner.
2. Work to build a positive self-concept.
3. Make a time commitment.
4. Remember that the teacher is the professional.
5. Don't pass the buck.
6. Stay in control.
7. Support each other.

PLANNING FOR A CONFERENCE

A parent-teacher conference is a short term purposeful exchange between a child's teacher and his/her parents. There are two major reasons for parent-teacher conferences. The first reason conferences are held is to obtain and/or convey information. The second reason is to solve a problem, the child's, the teacher's, or the parent's.

Either the parents or the teacher can initiate a conference. A mutually acceptable day, time, place, and length of time must be decided. During this initial contact, the purpose of the conference should be explained by the initiator.

Once the purpose is clear, both the parent and teacher can make the preparations that are necessary for a productive conference. Both the teacher and parents should prepare a list of questions that they intend to ask and topics they wish to discuss. Without a list, important topics are often forgotten and questions remain unanswered.

Parents should be prepared to provide information about the child's previous educational experiences, including the names of previous teachers, textbooks used, and grades received. The teacher may have questions about the child's activities at home, hobbies, and special interests. The teacher may also ask about other family members so that a more complete picture of the child can be obtained. Parents should be willing and prepared to share the disciplinary and management system used at home as this may be helpful to the teacher.

The teacher should be prepared to provide information about the child's educational and social progress. Therefore, the teacher should have at hand examples of the child's work in all major subjects, as well as significant test results. Additionally, peer relationships should be discussed. The teacher should be able to explain the child's strengths and limitations, always remembering to refrain from the use of educational jargon. It is helpful if teachers talk about exactly what the child is doing. For example, it is more helpful, if the teacher says that the child is currently performing simple addition and subtraction problems while the rest of the class is doing multiplication than to say that the child is a slow learner.

The key to a successful conference is prior planning. When the teacher and parents are organized and well-prepared for a conference, a great deal can be accomplished in a short amount of time. The form which follows can serve as an effective way for parents and teachers to prepare for conferences. Parents and teachers should attempt to complete it prior to a conference.

Form to Complete When Planning for a Conference
Purpose:

Day: _____

Time: _____

Place: _____

Length: _____

Significant information about child to share:

Topics to discuss and/or questions to ask:

Notes:

THE PROBLEM-SOLVING CONFERENCE

Most parent-teacher conferences are scheduled to discuss a problem. The problem may be one that either the teacher or parent or perhaps both have recognized.

After a suitable time and place have been established both the parent and the teacher should prepare for the conference. Both should be ready to specifically state the problem as it is perceived. The parent and teacher should try to not become defensive remembering that the problem will be best solved if they are working together.

If the parent has some ideas that may be helpful to the teacher, these should be shared in a cooperative manner. Teachers appreciate parent input when offered as possible alternatives rather than mandates for action. The parent must remember that the teacher has many other children demanding her attention.

The teacher should begin the conference with some positive comments about the student. Parents enjoy hearing good things about their children. Even though the conference is being held to discuss a problem situation, the teacher should initially say something positive about the child.

The teacher should never go to a conference without at least one constructive idea or suggestion about remedying the specific problem to be discussed. Prior to the conference the teacher (and the parents) should think about what is to be discussed and perhaps get some suggestions from colleagues. The teacher should try to enter the conference with several plans of action to propose; however, the alternate plans should not be offered until input from the parent has been obtained.

The best procedure for solving any problem is for the parent and teacher to work together. Use of the word "we" rather than "I" by both the parent and teacher tends to show this mutual support.

Once an intervention has been decided upon, it should be reviewed and any potential problems with implementing it should be discussed along with the action which will be taken when such problems arise. After discussion, the intervention should be written for both the parents and the teacher and perhaps the child, if appropriate.

If a problem has persisted for several months or perhaps even years, it is unrealistic to expect that it will be solved with only minimal effort. Parents and teachers should expect that they will have to modify plans and continue to cooperate and plan together in order to solve the problem. It is when parents and teachers plan together, persist, remain encouraged, don't place blame when plans don't work, and plan again if plans do not work, that children's problems in school have the best chance of being solved.

The following form could be used before and during a problem-solving conference. It could prove beneficial to both parents and teacher.

Complete Before the Conference

Date: _____

Time: _____

Place: _____

Length: _____

Participants:

Child: _____

Parent(s): _____

Teacher(s): _____

Others: _____

Statement of specific problem to be discussed:

Possible interventions:

Complete During the Conference

Notes:

Specific Intervention Agreed to Try:

Parent's responsibilities—

Teacher's responsibilities—

Child's responsibilities—

Responsibilities of others—

Things that may go wrong and contingency plans for dealing with these:

Scheduled follow-up:

TEACHER MORALE: WHAT TEACHERS
AND PARENTS CAN DO

The term "morale" can refer to several different aspects of a teacher's attitude about her position. It can refer to a teacher's mental and emotional response to the job (enthusiasm, dedication, etc.,); it can refer to a teacher's sense of common purpose with respect to the other professionals in the school; and it can refer to a teacher's general sense of well-being.

Morale is something which is unique to each individual teacher, and it is greatly affected by the people and things in the environment. A teacher's morale can be affected by her belief in the ability to positively influence the students, by the "esprit de corps" of colleagues at the school, by the physical condition of the school, by the support provided by the students' parents, and by many, many other factors.

For teachers to work effectively, morale needs to be as high as possible. Even when it is high, improvements in morale can lead to greater effectiveness. When morale is low, everyone suffers, with the students suffering the most.

There are many things that can be done to improve the morale of individuals and groups of teachers. Some things teachers need to do for themselves. Other things require effort from parents of students and others in the school environment. Any or all of the following people can do things to improve morale at a school: teachers, administrators, staff, parents, and students. The composition of the group, and whether it is a formal or informal group, are not important. What is done is the important thing.

The contributions that parents make are essential. At the most basic level, they can supervise their children to make sure homework gets completed and returned to school. They can also make sure their children have adequate learning materials, such as pens, pencils, and paper. If a teacher requests that the children bring in something for a special project, parents need to do what they can to make sure the materials are taken to school. Parents who have the time and resources to become more actively involved can volunteer to chaperone the students on field trips, serve as a teacher's aide, or tutor students. All of these things can improve teacher morale because they show the teacher that the parents also care about their children's learning and that they are willing to help in the process.

Joining the Parent-Teacher Organization is another way parents can show their support. This support can range from just joining the organization to becoming actively involved. Parent-Teacher Organizations often raise money to buy special equipment that schools could not otherwise afford. Just knowing that parents care enough to join can improve the morale of all the teachers at the school.

Teachers must realize that they do have very stressful and sometimes "thankless" jobs and it is important that they take measures to improve their outlook on what they are doing. If they do not assume this task of improving their morale, often no one else will, and the very best teachers will often "burnout" and lose enthusiasm for their jobs. What can teachers do to improve their morale?

1. Become Aware of Morale.

The very first thing that teachers should do is become aware that they should be concerned about their morale. Teachers must realize that how they feel about their jobs and the attitude they convey to students will influence their effectiveness. Teachers must be able to take a look at themselves and examine personal morale. If upon self-examination, morale is found to be low, teachers should take measures to improve it.

2. Establish a Support System.

Morale may be boosted when teachers have individuals or groups of other persons who are a support system for them. Often this support group is the teacher's family but it may be other teachers, administrators, professional organizations, clubs, sororities, etc. A support group provides a teacher with a means of venting professional and personal concerns and anxieties. Additionally, a support group will give a teacher motivation to make plans for improving morale if necessary. It is important for every teacher to remember that in addition to needing a support group, she should be a support person for other teachers — particularly young and inexperienced teachers.

3. Schedule Time for Self.

Most teachers become educators because they have a desire to help others. Sometimes this desire to be helpful results in a teacher not taking care of herself. Morale will improve when a teacher learns to engage in activities for herself and not feel guilty about this. At the top of the list of things to do for oneself is proper rest, nutrition, and exercise. Also, teachers should schedule "me" time, a period away from everyone to engage in an enjoyed activity — reading, relaxing, shopping, etc.

4. Gain New Skills.

Morale will remain high when teachers feel good about their ability to teach. All teachers must realize that there is always room for improvement in their teaching. Additionally, education in the 1980's is a rapidly changing field with many innovations and changes. In order to sustain high morale, teachers should view these changes and innovations as challenges and learn new skills for dealing with them. The list of new skills that may be acquired is endless and the skills acquired should depend upon the interest and motivation of the individual teacher.

5. Be Action Oriented.

Sometimes teachers will get caught in the trap of complaining about a problem in their school, with their students, or about the educational system in general. Complaining breeds complaining, and this energy could be much better spent doing something about the existing problem. A recent example of a group "doing something" about a problem was when local teachers applied for a high paying custodian's job at the local Post Office. Almost all teachers have complained about their poor salaries. This group took action and by example made a local and national impact on the public's view of the teacher salary issue. When teachers spend more time doing something about problems rather than complaining, morale should improve.

6. Be Positive.

Teachers need to realize that what human beings do is usually exactly what is done to them. Thus, when teachers are positive with administrators, students, parents, and other teachers, these individuals are much more likely to be positive toward the teacher. When a positive attitude is modeled by teachers in a school, that school is a much more pleasant environment for everyone—including the teachers.

If teacher morale is not high, students' learning will suffer. Therefore, it is important for teachers, parents, and other persons in the schools to be concerned about teacher morale and engage in activities to improve it. The suggestions which have been made for parents and teachers are just some of the possibilities which should prove successful.

THE IMPORTANCE OF EXPECTATIONS

Educational researchers studies the relationship between teacher expectations and student performance. In their research study, these investigators told teachers that one group of randomly selected students had low intellectual ability while a second randomly selected group had high intelligence. Throughout the school year students were tested and those with the reported low intelligence made less progress while those with the reported high ability made greatest gains. Thus, the teacher's expectations were confirmed by student performance.

Although Rosenthal and Jacobson's study has been criticized on statistical and design grounds, there have been many additional studies showing that teachers' positive and negative expectations do affect student behavior and test scores.

As the school year begins each teacher needs to examine critically his or her expectations of the children that he or she will be teaching. If a teacher expects John, who has a history of academic and behavior problems to create difficulty in the classroom, these expectations will be transmitted to John through verbal and nonverbal cues. And it is probable that these expectations for John will become a self-fulfilling prophecy.

John's teacher should have realistic expectations...neither those that are so great that John could never reach them nor those which are based on his past poor performance. Realistic expectations for John which include a plan of action for working with him should result in a positive experience for the teacher and John. It is best if teachers can view their "problems" as "challenges" and always attempt to meet the challenge!

Just as teachers' expectations influence student performance, students' expectations influence their own performance. Researchers conducted a study which investigated the relationship between children's expectations and their performance and found that elementary school childrens' perceptions of how they would perform mediated or influenced their actual performance. When the children thought they would fail, they usually did.

Parents influence to a large extent their childrens' perceptions of school. At the beginning of school, parents need to encourage their children to have positive expectations for the school year. If parents say, "I sure do hate to see school start," or "I have heard the school is in turmoil this year," these expectations are sure to influence those of their children.

To have a good beginning and a continued profitable educational experience, parents, teachers, and students should expect the best. Research, logic, and past experiences have proven that what we expect, usually happens.

EFFECTIVE COMMUNICATION
WITH CHILDREN

Teachers and parents interact with children hundreds of times each day. The process of quickly selecting appropriate responses is difficult, demanding and exhausting. Although arduous, communication is one of the most important aspects of effective teaching and parenting. Because communication is so important, parents and educators need to periodically examine the appropriateness and effectiveness of their interactions with children. The guidelines suggested by the authors are designed to assist teachers and parents in reviewing and evaluating communication with children.

1. Be Aware.

To effectively evaluate communication, teachers and parents must be able to hear and understand what is being said and how it is being received. One way to increase awareness is to make an audio tape. An analysis of the audio tape will help determine how often communication is positive, neutral or negative. Since there is a correlation between self-concept and positive communication, the goal is to increase positive feedback and communication. A second approach to becoming more aware is to ask for feedback; finding out if communication is clear and meaningful and questions are understandable. A third way to become more aware of communication is to imagine typical situations and visualize reactions. When a child says, "How shall I do this?" the teacher or parent may say, "do it this way," promoting dependence, or "What do you think?" encouraging autonomy, or "You don't remember we discussed that last week?" diminishing self-esteem. Whether using an audio tape, feedback or visualization, the first step to improved communication is becoming more aware.

2. Listen.

Who needs the most practice talking? Who gets the most practice? Unfortunately, most teachers and parents spend a lot more time talking than their children. When teachers or parents talk too much, children soon begin to not listen. Effective adult communicators promote student talk and then actively listen. To actively listen a teacher must hear and understand the child's words and the feelings expressed by the words and body language and let the child know she or he has been heard and understood by paraphrasing.

3. Question.

Effective cmmunicators know how to ask thought-provoking and open-ended questions. Open-ended questions such as, "What does evolution mean to you?" or "How are you feeling?" require discussion and interpretation, while closed questions such as, "Define evolution" or "Are you feeling bad" require a yes or no response or a memorized definition or answer. Unfortunately, many questions asked are closed. The goal should be to ask as many open-ended questions as possible and wait a sufficient amount of time for children to give quality responses.

4. Give Clear and Concise Directions.

A major portion of communication is giving directions. The biggest mistake made is giving too many directions at any one time. In addition to giving no more than three directions at a time, the following suggestions will help ensure that directions are understood and followed by students:

- Wait for children to attend before beginning.
- State the directions only once, because when directions are repeated several times, children will learn to wait for the repeated version before listening.
- Use specific words that state exactly what the children are expected to do and avoid words like "cooperate," "behave," or "think."

5. Send Consistent Messages.

Sometimes one thing is conveyed by the words while another contradicting message is indicated by body language and facial expression. Effective adult communicators use voice, body language and facial expression to send the same message. In addition to sending consistent messages, teachers and parents should use their voices only when necessary. If facial expression or body language is sufficient, avoid use of words.

6. Don't Be a Historian.

Some teachers and parents dredge up all past infractions when a child has violated a rule or made a mistake. This type of monologue is of no value and a waste of valuable time. Children (or anyone for that matter) can only deal with present behaviors. Nobody can correct his or her past. Teachers and parents should always attempt to deal with the present behavior and discuss history only as an academic subject.

The key to effective communication is to practice and evaluate. As teachers and parents become more aware of how they are communicating and use the suggested guidelines, communication will improve. As communication improves, students' self-confidence and achievement will also increase.

CHAPTER II

DISCIPLINE: A COOPERATIVE VENTURE

INTRODUCTION

MANY PARENTS and teachers associate the word "discipline" with punishment, or even corporal punishment, and this is incorrect. Discipline can refer to any procedure that is used to teach children how to behave in appropriate, acceptable ways. Because this is the main responsibilitiy of parents and teachers, discipline is a primary concern.

For discipline to be most effective, parents and teachers should work cooperatively to ensure that their children are making progress and experiencing success at home and in school. A prerequisite to this cooperation is a common vocabulary and common knowledge about appropriate procedures. The articles in this chapter were written to provide this common ground for parents and teachers.

The discipline techniques presented are based on the behavioral model. This model is concerned with people's observable behavior, and how that behavior is affected by consequences. Consequences are events or things that follow behavior and affect its future occurrence. Consequences that follow a behavior and increase its future occurrence are known as reinforcers. Consequences that follow a behavior and decrease its future occurrence are known as punishers. Parents and teachers are constantly using consequences, either consciously or not, to influence their children's behavior.

In this chapter we have tried to stress the importance of using positive, reinforcing consequences with children. It is in this way that children learn to become positive, productive members of the home and school community. We begin by explaining the basics of the behavioral approach to discipline in "What is Behavior Modification." This is followed by five articles on the use of reinforcement to ensure successful interactions with children. These articles are "The SPI Approach to Discipline," "Using Rewards Effectively," "Contingency Contracting, or Grandma's Law," "The Home-School Contract," and "Token Economies for Home and School."

Even the most positive parents and teachers must resort to the use of punishment, and this procedure is discussed in four articles. These are "How to Use Response Cost as Punishment," "Guidelines for Using Time Out," "Corporal Punishment: Reasons Not to Use It,"[1] and "The Criticism Trap."[2]

The final article is entitled "Your Discipline Quotient." This article includes two self-administered tests, one for parents, and one for teachers, that could be used for self-evaluation or to encourage discussion and communication.

It is hoped that these articles will help parents and teachers succeed in their cooperation venture of ensuring the positive growth of their children.

---

[1] Written by Dr. Robert Fowler, College of Charleston.
[2] Written by Dr. Chip Voorneveld, College of Charleston.

WHAT IS BEHAVIOR MODIFICATION?

Many parents and teachers have heard of "behavior modification" because it is frequently referred to in the educational literature, in books on how to raise children, and in newspapers and popular magazines. However, there still exists a great deal of confusion about what "behavior modification" is, and about its usefulness for parents and teachers.

When speaking of "behavior," we are talking about anything someone does that can actually be seen. The term "modification" means "change." Behavior modification, then, is the systematic use of behavioral principles and procedures to change behavior. The behavior may be our own or someone else's. These principles and procedures have been derived from the extensive scientific study of human behavior.

One basic behavioral principle is that a behavior that is followed by an experience the person considers pleasant will be more likely to be repeated in the future. Another basic behavioral principle is that a behavior that is followed by an experience a person considers unpleasant will be less likely to be repeated in the future.

An example of a basic procedure of behavior modification is direct observation and recording of the rate of a behavior (how often it occurs). By observing the rate of a behavior, it can be seen if any change has taken place because of a specific intervention.

Although it may not be obvious, all parents and teachers are using behavioral principles when teaching children new things, from how to make a bed to how to write a research paper. The difference between a "behaviorist" and a "non-behaviorist" is the systematic procedures used to teach new skills and change behaviors.

There are many misconceptions about behavior modification because people who are knowledgeable about the principles and procedures use the term inaccurately. Behavior modification does not include hypnosis, drug therapy or electro-convulsive shock, nor does it include psychoanalysis or any of the other types of therapy used today. Some people also associate behavior modification with coercive, punitive methods of control at one extreme or think that it is nothing more than the use of M & M candies at the other extreme.

What behavior modification is, is a very powerful, humane approach that can be used to help people learn new skills and new behaviors. Parents and teachers who want to learn more about the approach could find books in local libraries or bookstores.

THE "SPI" APPROACH TO DISCIPLINE

The elements of effective discipline are the same, whether they are used in a classroom, at home, or anywhere. It is also true that the mistakes a person can make when trying to discipline children are the same whether they are made by a teacher or a parent. In this article we present a very simple procedure to use when trying to improve the behavior of children at school and at home.

There are three basic steps to the "SPI" approach to effective discipline. They are:

1) **Specify**
2) **Praise**
3) **Ignore**

The first thing that parents and teachers need to do is to specify exactly what they expect the children to do, and how they expect them to do it. In the case of teachers, they very often specify the rules that the students are expected to follow. These rules should always be stated positively and should relate to specific behaviors. For example, "Walk in the halls," is much better than "Do not run in the halls." The guideline is to specify what children **should** be doing, not what they should not be doing.

Parents could also post rules, but more often they state their expectations for behavior. Again, these should be stated positively and relate to specific behaviors. For example, "Go to your room and make your bed," is better than "Don't make such a mess in your room."

Parents and teachers should communicate to ensure that the behaviors which are specified and required at home are comparable to those at school. Children, especially young children, often are confused when expectations vary from environment to environment.

After the teacher or parent specifies what is expected, and the child does what is expected, it is absolutely essential that the child is provided with some positive feedback about the appropriate behavior. This may come in the form of praise ("Good walking the halls!"), other verbal feedback ("Thank you for making your bed!"), a hug, a smile, or a pat on the back.

The last step in the "SPI" approach involves ignoring **minor** disruptions, or **minor** infractions of the rules. This is necessary because very often parents and teachers pay attention to children when they are misbehaving, rewarding the very behavior that they are trying to eliminate!

As is true when specifying behaviors, parents and teachers should communicate regarding the praising and ignoring of behaviors. This communication ensures that there is some consistency in discipline between home and school.

The beauty of the "SPI" approach is that it encourages teachers and parents to "Catch their children being good." Too often parents and teachers fall into the trap of ignoring children when they are good and only paying attention to them when they are bad. Children will do just about anything to get their parents' or teachers' attention. By using the "SPI" approach, parents and teachers can ensure that they are teaching children how to behave instead of how to misbehave.

USING REWARDS EFFECTIVELY

Parents and teachers often confuse the use of rewards or reinforcers with bribery. When it is suggested that free time be awarded for assignments completed, a teacher might think of this as a bribe. When it is suggested that children be given money (their allowance) for completion of chores, a parent might think of this as a bribe.

Actually, bribery is the misuse of rewards. If a person is offered a reward (usually money) for doing something that is illegal, immoral, or dishonest, that is a bribe. A person is being encouraged to do something that should not be done. Obviously, people who use the word "bribe" to refer to rewards given to children for appropriate behavior need to consult their dictionary.

Another misconception about rewards is that they should not be given for behaviors that "we expect of" our children. For some reason some parents and teachers believe that if children are expected to complete their classroom assignments and do their chores at home, they should not expect rewards. We wonder if these adults would do their jobs without expecting rewards (paychecks) for their accomplishments.

In truth, people need reasons for doing many of the things they do. This is known as motivation. We know of few adults who would contrive to work without the motivation supplied by a paycheck. Children also need to be motivated by the promise of rewards and recognition for the work they do at home and at school. Appropriate rewards for children will not spoil them anymore than a paycheck spoils their parents and teachers.

There are many ways teachers and parents can recognize, reward, and motivate children. They can use social reinforcers, which are words spoken or written ("Good job of making your bed." "Thank you for playing quietly."), facial expressions (a smile, a wink), or bodily expressions (clapped hands, a thumbs up sign). All these things show approval and recognize a job well done.

Adults can also reward children with access to activities. Teachers can use recess or free time, quiet talking, running errands, clapping the erasers, etc. Parents can use television or telephone time, time with friends, outside activities, etc. This list of activity reinforcers is almost endless; furthermore, they are usually free.

The last category of rewards that adults can make available are tangible, or things that children can touch and feel. Examples are pencils, paper, food, physical contact, money, toys, etc. In this category we find the most powerful reinforcers.

The following guidelines should be followed when using rewards at home and in school.

1. Remember that difficult children find different things reinforcing. One child may love recess time, another may love quiet time in the room.
2. Never use a reward that is more powerful than necessary. Do not give toys when smiles and praise are enough.
3. The reward should always be given after the behavior, not before. Do not give a child dessert in return for a promise to eat his or her peas after dessert is finished.
4. The reward should be directly linked to the appropriate behavior. For example, "You may go outside to play because you have finished your work," relates the reward to the behavior.
5. The reward should follow the appropriate behavior as soon after it happens as possible. If there is a delay, bridge it with an explanation.
6. Do not use the same rewards over and over again. Variety increases their effectiveness.
7. The number of rewards given is important, and varies from child to child. Do not be afraid of giving too much. That error is better than giving too little.

By using rewards for appropriate behavior, and by following these guidelines, teachers and parents will encourage their children's progress. The positive nature of interaction using rewards also improves relationships between the adults and children. Any adults wishing to improve the quality of their interaction with children could complete the following worksheet. The worksheet can be completed with individual children or whole groups in mind.

USING REWARDS EFFECTIVELY

Social Rewards (Things the adult can say to recognize appropriate behavior)

Used Often:

Additional Ones That Could Be Used:

Activity Rewards (Things the children like to do)

Used Often:

Additional Ones that Could Be Used:

Tangible Rewards (Things the adult can give children)

Used Often:

Additional Ones That Could Be Used:

CONTINGENCY CONTRACTING, OR "GRANDMA'S LAW"

The best techniques to use when disciplining children are (1) positive, (2) simple, (3) used consistently, and (4) lead to self-management and self-control. One technique that meets all these criteria is called "contingency contracting." If this term sounds too complicated, it can also be called "Grandma's Law" which is, "When you finish your dinner, you may have your dessert."

In essence, the parent or teacher makes engaging in one activity contingent upon completion of another activity. In other words, the parent or teacher says, "When you do X, then you may do Y." Obviously for this to work, the child must want to do Y.

The opportunities to use this technique are almost endless. In the classroom, the teacher might say, "When you finish your math, you may go to recess," or "When you hand in your papers, you may read whatever you want." At home, the parent might say, "When you make your bed, you may go outside," or "When you finish your homework, you may watch TV."

Too often, instead of allowing children to earn their enjoyable activities for doing something right, parents and teachers take away enjoyable activities for doing something wrong. Another mistake is allowing children to first do what they want to do in hopes they will then do what they do not want to do. But if the very simple technique, "When X then Y," is used, parents and teachers are teaching children how to behave instead of how not to behave.

Parents and teachers would also be wise to apply contingency contracting to their own lives. For example, a teacher could say, "When I finish grading these papers, I'll go call my best friend on the phone." A parent might say, "When I'm finished with these dishes, I'll watch my favorite TV show." By following something we don't want to do with something we want to do, we are accentuating the positive in our own lives also.

THE HOME-SCHOOL CONTRACT

When problems arise at school, the best solutions usually involve both parents and the teacher. This joint effort is more likely to lead to success than if the teacher or the parents work independently of one another.

One problem solving tool that can be used by the teacher and the parents is known as a "home-school contract." A home-school contract can be useful in solving such problems as tardiness, failure to complete homework assignments, or failure to complete assignments in class.

The home-school contract has four components and a possible fifth bonus clause. The components are:

1. Specification of the child's classroom responsibilities and the behaviors that will lead to a reward.
2. Specification of the reward to be earned.
3. Specification of what will happen if the child does not live up to the contract.
4. Specification of the system that will be used to monitor the child's progress.
5. Specification of possible bonuses for going beyond the contract's specifications.

What differentiates the home-school contract from other contract is the fact that the reward is awarded at home by the parents. The rewards that are available at home are often more meaningful to the child than those that are available at school. Possible rewards include television time, outside playtime, being able to have a friend stay overnight, a special food treat, and tickets to the movies or roller skating. The choice of the reward should be based on what the child enjoys. Input from the child will ensure the selection of an appropriate reward.

Obviously, the teacher and parents must have a good system of communication established in order to successfully implement a home-school contract. The teacher and parents must stipulate dates for a review of contract results and agree to procedures for changing the contract. The monitoring system must be clearly specified in order for the contract to be functional.

After a contract has been written, signatures should indicate agreement. All parties involved in the contract should sign it. To enhance communication and ensure clarity, copies of the contract should be given to all persons who signed it.

If the home-school contract is not a success, it is recommended that changes be made in the contract. Any one of the five components can be changed to ensure success. Keep the contract as simple as possible, the reward as meaningful as possible, and the monitoring system as functional as possible, and the chances will be good that the contract will make a difference.

The following form gives an example of a home-school contract. Guidelines to follow in writing the contract are included in each section.

School's Name
Home-School Contract

Between _____ (Student), _____ (Teacher), and _____ (Parent).

Student's Responsibility

(Guidelines:

1. Be very specific about the behavior expected.
2. List the steps or components of the behavior if it is lengthy or complicated.
3. Make sure the student understands the responsibilities.
4. Specify date(s) of completion.
5. Keep the responsibilities as simple and basic as possible.)

Reward to be Earned at Home for Fulfilling the Responsibility

(Guidelines:

1. This must be something the student wants and must earn.
2. Ask for student's opinion.
3. Be sure not to "inflate" the reward by offering too much, or "deflate" by offering too little.
4. The reward can be broken into steps or components if the student's expected behavior is lengthy or complicated.
5. The parent **must** agree to award the reward when earned, no matter what else the student has done (or not done).

Consequences for Not Fulfilling Responsibility

(Guidelines:

1. This could be simple—If the student does not meet the contract requirements, the reward is not given.
2. Parents **must** agree not to award the reward if it is not earned as specified in the contract.
3. The contract should be re-written to ensure success the next time.)

System to Monitor Progress and Communicate Between Home and School

(Guidelines:

1. The person(s) responsible for monitoring +communication must be clear.
2. A system and procedure must be developed.
3. Student self-monitoring should be built in if possible.)

Possible Bonus (Optional)

(Guidelines:

1. Same as for "Rewards"
2. The Bonus should be for Student's completion of responsibilities "above and beyond" the contract.)

Signatures

We, the undersigned, understand all the components of this contract, and agree to our roles and responsibilities:

_____ (Student)   _____ Date

_____ (Teacher)

_____ (Parent)

_____ (Others)

TOKEN ECONOMIES IN HOME AND SCHOOL

Teachers and parents who are looking for a potentially powerful procedure to use to teach children appropriate behaviors might consider the use of a token economy. This very positive procedure can be used in the classroom or at home, with individual children or whole groups. In this type of system, points or tokens are given to children for specific appropriate behaviors, and they exchange these points or tokens for activities or things they want.

For example, each assignment completed in the classroom is worth one point. Ten points can be exchanged for ten minutes of free time. At home, each time a child makes the bed, one point is awarded. Ten points can be exchanged for five minutes on the telephone.

The following steps should be followed when setting up a token economy:

1) The adult and child should decide and agree on the behavior that will earn tokens. The behavior should be very specific and understood by everyone. It is best to start with just one.
2) An easy way to record whether the child has earned a token must be established.
3) A decision must be made about what tokens should be used. Points, stars, chips, pennies, or holes punched in a card can be used.
4) The reward should be decided on. This must be something the child could not otherwise do or have, and that is very desirable.
5) The "pay" for the behavior, and the "cost" of the reward should be decided on. Care should be given not to inflate or deflate the economy.

This highly structured system will work well if it is implemented with care and consistency. It takes a commitment of time from the parents and teachers, but the results can be astounding. One of the greatest benefits is that adults are teaching children what they should be doing, and giving them a reason for doing it. Being positive is always the best way to accomplish anything.

An example of a token economy follows. The student's responsibilities, the "pay" for completing them, and the rewards and their "price" are all included. Points are recorded on the sheet by the parents for the first two behaviors, and by the teacher for the third. It would be best if initials or signatures be used so that the points would not be "counterfeited" by the student. The student could earn 40 points for a perfect week, but there are rewards available for less than perfect performance. This helps to ensure success each week. It should be noted that the rewards are all activities that do not cost anyone any money. The rewards could also have been given at home, as in a home-school contract.

As the student makes progress the "prices" of rewards could be raised to encourage growth. It is probable that the student would be the first to suggest that the system be phased out, that it is no longer needed. However, if problems should arise again, the token economy could be used.

Ronald's
Token Economy

Responsitilities and points that can be earned:

#1. All homework assignments taken home - 2 points
#2. All necessary books, etc. taken home - 2 points
#3. Completed homework returned to school - 4 points

	Assignments Home	Books Home	Returned School	Total
Monday				
Tuesday				
Wednesday				
Thursday				
Friday				
Total for the Week				

Rewards to be traded for on Friday afternoon:

Free Time
   10 minutes   20 points
   20 minutes   40 points
Choose recess activities for next week   30 points
Line Leader for next week   30 points

HOW TO USE RESPONSE COST
AS PUNISHMENT

Any teacher who has taken recess away from a student has used response cost. Any parent who has taken television watching privileges away from a child has used response cost. Any adult who has been given a traffic ticket and a fine has had response cost used on them. It would probably be impossible to find a teacher, parent, or policeman who has not used this procedure in an attempt to punish someone for some misdeed.

Response cost is a punishment procedure. In this procedure, following a misdeed of some sort, the adult takes something away from the child that the child likes. The adult can take away, for a specified period of time, access to an activity that the child likes, such as recess, playing with friends, or talking on the telephone. Tangible items can also be taken away, such as toys, comic books, or games. In the case of the adult who receives a traffic ticket, she or he has money taken away after breaking a rule.

The key to the effective use of response cost is making sure what is taken away is actually of value to the person being punished. A child who does not like to go to recess might actually misbehave in order to stay in the classroom. Conversely, a child who loves recess would find this procedure very unpleasant. As another example, a very rich person would not be affected by a traffic fine, whereas a poor person would be.

As with the use of all types of punishment, the loss should fit the misdeed. A child who fails to make his bed in the morning might lose a half hour of television, but not a whole week's worth. A student who blurts out an answer in class might lose five minutes of recess, but not the whole period.

The loss of the activity or item should also follow this misbehavior as closely as possible. This way the teacher or parent can be sure that they are punishing the behavior they want to decrease in frequency. Delay can result in the punishment of a behavior that may actually need to be increased in frequency.

Children might also be given the opportunity to earn back things they have lost. This gives them an opportunity to practice the correct behavior, and receive rewards. It also encourages the child to return to the adult for the reinforcement, thereby strengthening a relationship that may have been weakened because of the need for punishment.

Ideally, children should be given the opportunity to earn their activities and items they like, rather than be threatened with their loss if they misbehave. As an example, it is much better for a teacher to say, "When you finish your work, you may go to recess," than to say, "If you don't finish your work, I won't let you go to recess." Parents would find it much more effective if they said, "When you finish your homework, you may watch TV," rather than, "No TV for you unless you finish your homework." As usual, positive procedures are the best.

USING "TIME OUT" AT HOME AND SCHOOL

Any parent who has sent a child to his or her room as a form of punishment has used time out. Any teacher who has sent a child to the hallway as a form of punishment has used time out. Obviously, there is nothing new or unusual about this procedure.

"Time out" is an abbreviation for "time out from positive reinforcement." For the procedure to be successful, the child must be removed from place "A" where there is the opportunity for positive reinforcement, and be sent to place "B" where positive reinforcement is not available. In other words the child must want to be in place "A" (the living room with the rest of the family, the classroom with friends) and not want to be in the other (the bedroom, the hallway). If this is not the case, time out is not being used.

Time out, when used correctly, is a very powerful form of punishment. Guidelines should be followed so that abuse does not occur. We suggest that the following guidelines be followed at home and school:

1) The child should know the exact reason s/he is being sent to time out. The inappropriate behavior should be specified.
2) The time spent in time out should be brief, about 5 to 10 minutes. This is especially true in a classroom because this time is taken from classroom instruction and learning.
3) The place used as time out should be neutral, with adequate lighting, ventilation, heat, etc. We would suggest that a child's bedroom **not** be used for time out because the bedroom will be associated with punishment.
4) Time out should be one component of a total management program that emphasizes the use of reinforcement to teach appropriate behaviors.

If parents and teachers decide to use time out, records should be kept. The inappropriate behavior should be described, including the date and time of day, and things that happened before and after. The amount of time spent in time out should be noted also. Because this information is being recorded, it will be obvious if this procedure is working to reduce the frequency of unacceptable behavior. If the frequency is not decreasing, then this is not an effective procedure for

the child. Parents and teachers must guard against the mistake of using a procedure that they think is working, but really is not.

As one final check, the parent or teacher must be sure that the
child has access to positive reinforcement in place "A" and that this is
not available in place "B." In other words, the child should find more
pleasure in the classroom than the hallway, and more joy with the
family than alone.

CORPORAL PUNISHMENT: REASONS FOR NOT USING IT

Parents and teachers have used corporal punishment for many years. It is almost a given that children will be "spanked," "whipped," or "paddles" for rule infractions. Behaviors which may cause the child to be corporally punished range from something as simple as refusing to eat vegetables, to more serious transgressions. Obviously, most adults do not corporally punish children because they really dislike them. They hit children for a variety of reasons. Some have not really thought about what they are doing; others just do not know a better way (or at least they think that they do not know); and many really believe that they are doing what is in the best interests of the child. The purpose of this article is to explore some of the reasons why people corporally punish children and to outline reasons for not using this form of control with children.

The situation in which parents and teachers often find themselves can be a frustrating one. Children, just being themselves, are often unavoidably going to behave in a manner which is unacceptable to adults. Oftentimes, they are just "rulebreakers" and at other times they do something which is dangerous to themselves or others. In any event, something must be done to let them know that their behavior is unacceptable. All too often, the first response of an adult is to deal with the behavior in an emotional, rather than logical, manner. People often overreact to the situation and use punitive measures which do not really fit the transgression. The result of all of this is confrontation and confusion.

Here is an example of this: the same child is dragged down the same hall by the same teacher, day after day, to be paddled by the same principal for the same offense, or; the same child is spanked by the same parent, day after day, for the same violation. Why, then, all the sames? Could it just be that something is not working? Could it be that the adults in charge might want to try another way? Of course, the answer to both questions is yes. However, in order for these questions to be answered and another solution arrived at, it is necessary to look at what is going on and determine why people behave the way they do. Although the corporal punishment is not really working, it appears to be working if the situation is not carefully analyzed. In the first circumstance, the teacher is reinforced by the temporary termination of the behavior in question. The behavior stops, but it is likely that the attention received from the teacher and the other children in the class is very reinforcing for the child. All of a sudden, the child is the focus of attention. Even with the threat of being punished by the principal, the attention is most rewarding. This of course is not always true for all children, but it is in many cases.

Now, what about the trip to the office? Depending on how the child makes the trip to the office, the potential for reinforcement is tremendous. If the child is sent on his/her own, stand by. Unless the classroom is right by the principal's office, the trip may be a long and time-consuming one. The child has the opportunity to visit with all sorts of people (other children, teachers, the custodian, etc.) and receive more attention from them. By the time s/he arrives at the office, the child may have become somewhat of a celebrity. Once inside the office, again, the potential for reinforcement is great. Just imagine all of the people from whom the child could receive support and sympathy while waiting to be punished by the "mean old principal." (Conjure up in your mind the pathetic picture a misty-eyed child about to be paddled could present.) By the time the principal begins to dispense the punishment, a great deal of time has passed and the child has almost forgotten about the original infraction. Also, the child will have been reinforced by the attention gained from the principal. After the administration of the paddling the child is released to return to the classroom, wearing a badge of courage and bragging about how many "licks" were taken without shedding a tear. The same principles apply in the case of the child being corporally punished by the parent. Those principles are: (1) attention is reinforcing for the child, and (2) the momentary cessation of the unacceptable behavior is reinforcing to the adult in charge. The bottom line is: Behaviors (appropriate or inappropriate) exist because they are reinforced.

Now that it is known why people continue to use corporal punishment even though it is not effective and even though there are better ways to help children in the management of their behavior, let us take a look at some reasons for not using corporal punishment. (There are numerous alternatives in this book, all of which are simple, efficient, and effective.) The following list should convince anyone, but it is by no means an exhaustive one.

Reasons For Not Using Corporal Punishment

1. CORPORAL PUNISHMENT LEADS TO THE ESTABLISHMENT OF AVOIDANCE BEHAVIORS. Children who are corporally punished learn to avoid persons who hit them. Let us face it. It hurts (physically and psychologically) when you are hit. Most adults do not like being hit and they will not tolerate it from others. Most of us just do not enjoy pain and we will do all we can to avoid it. If we feel a headache coming on, we take a pain reliever to avoid having the headache. If we meet someone who causes us embarrassment or some other kind of psychological pain we tend to avoid that person in the future. The biggest problem corporally punished children face is that they normally cannot avoid the adult who hits them. Like it or not, they must be around the people who hit them. And that is frustrating to the child.

2. THE USE OF CORPORAL PUNISHMENT LEADS TO THE ESTABLISHMENT OF ESCAPE BEHAVIORS. Above, it is mentioned that children will try to avoid those who corporally punish them. Along with this is the occurrence of attempts to escape from the punisher. It is easy to see why the child would want to do so. If one is faced with the inevitability of the situation, then the last resort is escape — by whatever means. It is not uncommon to observe adults chasing young children in order to administer corporal punishment. Perhaps the only reason that older children do not try to escape (run) is that they have learned that the severity of the punishment will indeed be much greater if a escape attempt is made. As in the case of the establishment of avoidance behavior, it is usually not the intention of the adult in a position of authority to have children avoid them or to try to escape from them.

3. THE USE OF CORPORAL PUNISHMENT PROVIDES A MODEL FOR AGGRESSION. When a child is corporally punished, s/he quickly learns that under certain circumstances it is acceptable to hit. The rule learned is that hitting is permissible if the one doing the hitting is bigger or in a position of authority over another. In other words, the use of corporal punishment actually

teaches physical aggression. All of us, consciously or otherwise, imitate the behavior of those around us. Children are particularly vulnerable to this process, especially when they are around adults whom they respect. This is extraordinarily important in the case of parents and teachers. Parents and teachers are significant adults in the lives of children and they tend to model the behaviors they see displayed by a parent or a teacher. So, what we have is a situation in which children learn physical agression from very powerful figures in their lives.

4. THE USE OF CORPORAL PUNISHMENT ESTABLISHES FEAR IN THE CHILD. There are, of course, situations and people whom children should fear (e.g. strangers, busy streets). However, it is absurd to think that people would espouse a philosophy which would encourage parents and teachers to have children learn to fear them. Therefore, it is reasonable to assume that the fear which is learned is done inadvertently merely because people have not closely examined what they are doing. Thus, the by-products of the use of corporal punishment are fear and anxiety. Neither of these make positive contributions to the healthy development of a child.

5. SOCIETY'S PERMISSIVE ATTITUDE REGARDING THE USE OF CORPORAL PUNISHMENT IS LINKED TO CHILD ABUSE. It has been well established that when children are corporally punished for a recurring behavior, the punishment becomes increasingly severe with each successive administration. Further, the spanking is generally done while the adult is in an emotional "state" which clouds objectivity. It is therefore easy to understand how harmful, both physically and psychologically, the punishment can become in a very short period of time. Those who use something other than the open hand in administration of corporal punishment are most likely to become child abusers. The use of sticks, belts, extension cords, brushes, or other devices is quite obviously unnecessary and patently wrong. Child abusers do not start out to inflict physical harm and pain; the predicament just gets out of hand quickly.

6. CORPORAL PUNISHMENT SUPPRESSES BEHAVIOR RATHER THAN CHANGING IT. The intention of the punisher is to change the behavior of the child. With corporal punishment, however, it is generally the case that the behavior is suppressed in

the presence of the punisher, rather than being changed. Given a situation in which the adult is absent, the child will behave in the same way. Essentially, the child has not learned the "lesson" which was to have been taught.

7. CORPORAL PUNISHMENT PROVIDES NO INFORMATION REGARDING HOW TO BEHAVE. Children are typically spanked, paddled, or hit immediately following the violation and infrequently learn other ways to behave. They may learn about what caused them to be punished, but they do not gain information as to what they could have done differently. Even in the case of a discussion which follows the delivery of the punishment it is doubtful that any child is capable of being objective enough to overlook the pain and embarrassment in order to think about substitute behaviors.

8. THE USE OF CORPORAL PUNISHMENT IS NOT ETHICAL. Childhood is admittedly a relatively recent invention. Children used to be thought of as property which could be sold or dealt with in almost any manner. Now, thankfully, we have progressed to the point where some kind of respect is being afforded to children. Labor laws protect children; the old sweat shops are fortunately a thing of the past. Laws regarding child abuse are becoming increasingly better. Several years ago, Sweden passed a law prohibiting the corporal punishment of children. Even parents are not allowed to corporally punish their children. It is encouraging that some people are seriously responding to the need to respect the rights of children. What we are talking about is simple respect for the dignity and worth of a human being. In the final analysis, corporal punishment is embarrassing, demeaning, and demoralizing. It is ludicrous to think that adults would allow others to treat them in a similar manner. How people can justify treating children otherwise is indeed mystifying.

In summary, there are a number of reasons for not using corporal punishment in the management of children. Any one of the reasons just listed is sufficient for the cessation of the practice. It is not suggested that one stop using a method of management without substituting other methods. The other procedures include, but are not limited to: positive reinforcement for appropriate behaviors, time-out, response cost, and the reinforcement of incompatible behaviors. All of these procedures are explained in detail elsewhere in this book. The procedures are effective, efficient, and are easily learned. Using these better ways to help children manage their own behavior (and this should be the ultimate goal of any management system) will produce amazing results in a very short period of time. Even more importantly, though, the better ways will help everyone involved to manage the daily routines of life in a calmer, saner, and more positive manner. It is not implied that life will be without problems from this moment on. It is, nonetheless, held that parents and teachers who do abandon the use of corporal punishment and adopt the more positive and effective methods suggested will experience a significant and positive change in their interaction with children. Everyone benefits.

ARE YOU CAUGHT IN THE "CRITICISM TRAP?"

Parents and teachers have often heard the saying, "You can catch more flies with honey than you can with vinegar." This maxim can be applied to children's behavior as well as that of flies if we think of the honey as praise, and the vinegar as criticism. Translated into a maxim for parents and teachers the result is, "Children behave more appropriately when you use praise than when you use punishment." If this is true, then why do some parents and teachers use more criticism than praise when trying to influence children's behavior? The answer is that they are caught in the "Criticism Trap."

Parents and teachers get caught in the Criticism Trap if (1) they tend to ignore children when they are being good, and (2) they attend to children when they are being bad. Unfortunately, it is relatively easy to get into the trap, because children usually do stop, at least temporarily, their annoying inappropriate behavior when verbally reprimanded by a parent or teacher. Because they stop, the parent or teacher is actually reinforced for reprimanding, and will probably do it again in the future. What the adult does not understand, though, is that the reprimand was actually a reward for the child! This is because the child who gets little or no positive feedback about correct behavior is willing to put up with a reprimand (or even harsher punishment) rather than get no attention at all from the parent or teacher. The cycle becomes endless: a child is ignored when good, but desires adult attention; the child then misbehaves to get the attention; the parent or teacher thinks punishment is being used when the child is reprimanded because the reprimand stops the behavior for a while; this rewards the adult, but it also rewards the child who will repeat the misdeed for further adult attention.

By clearly seeing what is going on, the teacher or parent can avoid the "Criticism Trap" and behave in ways that will produce the desired long-range effects of shaping children's appropriate behavior. This can best be done by reinforcing desired behavior and ignoring minor disruptions. The answer sounds simple but its implementation can be difficult. Honey (praise) is the key word. Parents and teachers must always try to remember to catch children being good! Catch them being good on the playground, in the classroom, at their desks, at the dinner table, playing with their siblings, in the family car, and at any time that appropriate behavior is observed. Once teachers and parents catch children being good, they are reinforcing desired behavior, and once this behavior has been reinforced, the adults have increased the probability that the behavior will occur again. These behaviors can be reinforced by using praise, winks, "Thank you," and any of the other ways discussed in the articles in this chapter.

Of course, catching children being good does not happen without a great deal of practice and concentration on the part of parents and teachers, especially if they have been caught in the "Criticism Trap" for long. It can be difficult for adults to look at a situation and admit that the problem is really theirs and not the children's. Take the example of the child in school who constantly calls out. It would be simple to say, "Stop calling out," every time the child does this. It would be more difficult to turn that thinking around and ignore the child when she calls out and praise her when she raises her hand. It takes patience and practice for adults to reverse their habits. However, with practice parents and teachers can become more positive and escape the "Criticism Trap."

The following six methods could be used by parents or teachers if they desire to either avoid the "Criticism Trap," or to escape it. Also remember that anything that is done that will help the parent or teacher increase praise and decrease criticism will benefit the children as well as the adults.

1. Use reminders to praise more, such as signs or other prompts.
2. Practice praising. The more it is done the easier it becomes.
3. Make it possible to be reinforced for praising more. Usually, the improvement in the child's behavior is a good reinforcer for parents and teachers.
4. Use key thoughts such as "Catch Them Being Good" as a mental reminder.
5. Do not require perfection before rewarding children. Reward small improvement for best results.
6. When calling attention to a child's appropriate behavior, be specific about what was dne to warrant approval.

When parents and teachers make a concerted effort to increase the number of times they reinforce children for appropriate behavior and ignore minor disruptions, their interactions with children will greatly improve. Using these simple suggestions will help adults break out of the "Criticism Trap."

YOUR "DISCIPLINE QUOTIENT"

The American Heritage Dictionary defines "discipline" as "training that is expected to produce a specified character or pattern of behavior, especially that which is expected to produce moral or mental improvement." This training is one of the major responsibilities of all parents and teachers, and as such, is always an area of mutual concern. As parents and teachers interact with children, the discipline techniques that they use can be either complimentary or they can work at cross purposes. Obviously, when the adults work together, the children will benefit.

Unfortunately, the discipline of children is a topic that can be a major source of disagreement between husbands and wives, and between parents and teachers. Often the root of the problem is that these adults have not given a great deal of systematic thought to the subject, and consequently their approaches to discipline are fragmented and inconsistent. Discussion can lead to argument, with the children being the losers.

In an attempt to facilitate discussion about discipline between husbands and wives, or parents and teachers, we have designed two parallel evaluation forms, one for parents and one for teachers. They could be used for self-evaluation or to provide the impetus for discussion between spouses, or parents and teachers.

To be most useful, the questions, which are located at the end of this article, should be answered before reading further. It will take about five minutes to complete the questions, all of which relate directly to the essential components of a behavior management system.

After completing the evaluation, check the answers as you read about each component. Score 1 point for each "Yes" and 0 points for each "No." A score of 3 in any component is excellent, 2 is fair, and 1 or 0 needs improvement. Instructions for interpretation of the total score is at the end of the article.

I. Have a Philosophy of Discipline.

Questions 1, 2, and 3   Your Score _____

The first component of effective discipline is a philosophy of, or approach to, the management of children. There are many widely publicized aproaches to discipline, including behavior modification,

Reality Therapy, Transactional Analysis, Parent Effectiveness Training and Teacher Effectiveness Training. Most parents and teachers instinctively choose parts of these approaches, combining what they have learned through reading, talking with other parents and teachers, and through trial and error.

One way to determine a philosophy is to attempt to write it down. The statements do not need to be elaborate; three or four sentences or phrases could succinctly describe a person's approach to the discipline of children. It would also be helpful for parents to share this with one another, or parents and teachers to share their responses. This could provide an opportunity for clarification and cooperation.

There are no "right" or "wrong" philosophies, but writing it down will make it much easier to implement an effective discipline system. Also, by writing this philosophy and sharing it with other adults it will help ensure a greater degree of consistency in the management of children. A well thought-out philosophy is the keystone of an effective approach to discipline. Ultimately, this philosophy should be one that is meaningful, practical, and beneficial to the adults and the children.

II. Specify the Rules

Questions 4, 5 and 6   Your score _____

One of the major tasks of childhood is to learn how to behave in different situations with different people. The primary responsibility for teaching this to children rests with parents and teachers. Consequently, the adults can make this task easier for children by being very specific about how children are expected to behave. Teachers usually do this by specifying rules that are to be followed in the classroom, or by verbal explanation. Parents usually do this by explaining to their children how they are expected to behave.

Unfortunately, many adults punish their children for breaking rules that were never fully explained, or even stated at all. An example would be a student who gets reprimanded for not lining up properly, when the teacher never specified how she or he wanted that done. A child who gets reprimanded for having the radio on too loud, but "too loud" was never explained by the parents, is also being punished unfairly.

Ideally, the expectations adults have for the children's behavior should be perfectly clear to the children. These expectations, or rules should always be stated positively so that the children are learning how to behave, instead of how not to behave. For example, "Walk in the halls" is a much better rule than, "Don't run in the halls." "Make your bed every morning before school," is far superior to "Don't be so messy." By stating the expectations clearly, and showing children how to meet these expectations if necessary, parents and teachers can make learning much easier for children.

When rules and expectations are stated positively, it is relatively easy for parents and teachers to be positive and reinforcing with children. Conversely, when rules and regulations are stated negatively, it is very easy to be overly critical. This is an additional reason for specifying rules that tell children what they are supposed to do.

III. Be Positive

Questions 7, 8, and 9   Your score _____

Given the choice between "happy" and "sad," almost all people would choose "happy." Given the choice between "pleasant" and "unpleasant," almost all would choose "pleasant." Mysteriously, many adults do not choose the happy, pleasant alternative of "positive," over the sad, unpleasant alternative of "negative" when they discipline children.

There are many benefits to using a positive approach to discipline, and the adults and children would reap them. Children are recognized for their correct behavior, and consequently are more likely to behave correctly again. This increases their chances for more pleasant interactions with adults. The children are also being taught how to behave, and what to do, rather than what not to do.

Adults also benefit because the children are behaving correctly and making life much easier for the adults. The maxim that "What you send out comes back to you," is very evident in this situation. As adults become more positive with children, all the good that is inherent in this approach returns to the adult. Being nice always pays off.

IV. If Punishment is Necessary, Be Fair.

Questions 10, 11, and 12   Your score _____

It is even possible to be positive when punishment is called for. Minor disruptions should be ignored as long as the parent or teacher is continuing to reinforce children for correct behavior. If ignored, minor disruptions are likely to decrease in frequency as the children learn correct behavior through the use of reinforcement. (A word of caution is needed here: All the ignoring in the world will not help if children get attention for their inappropriate behavior from other adults or children.)

It is necessary to note that one adult's minor disruption can be another's major infraction, and punishment may be necessary. In these cases, it is important to remember to make sure the punishment fits the "crime." Adults who punish frequently, and use harsh forms of punishment often find that they must continuously increase the "dose." This will be particularly true if the adult fails to give adequate amounts of positive feedback to the child.

Adults should always try to be fair when punishing a child. If a teacher or parent takes away a privilege, the child should have an opportunity to earn it back. If a reprimand is called for, the adult should calmly specify what the child did wrong, and briefly describe the correct behavior. In these ways, children are given the opportunity to learn from their mistakes, and have the chance to experience future success.

V. Be Consistent

Questions 13, 14 and 15   Your score _____

Specifying the rules, praising, ignoring minor disruptions, and punishing when necessary are excellent procedures to follow when disciplining children. However, one more component is necessary, and that is consistency. Keeping in mind a child's natural development as she or he gets older, today's rules should also be tomorrow's rules. A child should not have to guess about an adult's expectations, and the adult should not expect the child to read his or her mind.

In addition, parents and teachers should try to remain as consistent as possible in their responses to children. If adults are not consistent, children begin to play a guessing game. "If Teacher is in a good mood, maybe I can get away with this." "I wonder if Mom will be pleased about my good grade?" "I wonder what will happen if I don't come home on time?" "I wonder how many times I can do this before Dad gets mad." It is not the child's fault if these games begin. Being consistent keeps the game from starting.

VI. Be a Good Model.

Question 16   Your score _____
(Give yourself 3 for a yes on this one)

It would be possible that if parents and teachers were always perfect, their children would be also. Since there is no chance of that happening, the best we can strive for is to provide a model of behavior that we would want children to emulate. If we want them to be nice to other people, we must be nice to other people. If we want them to respect us, we must respect them. Many behaviors, whether good or bad, are learned through a modeling process, and parents and teachers are the primary role models in young children's lives. Often what parents and teachers do, rather than what they say, teaches children how to behave.

Conclusions

To determine your overall "Discipline Quotient" count your total number of "yes" responses and record this number on your test. Compare this total score with the ranges below:

      15 - 16   Excellent
      13 - 14   Good
      11 - 12   Fair
      Below 11   Needs Improvement

The value of this assessment is not in the score itself, but in its ability to prompt a change in your approach to discipline, if necessary. If you want to improve your score and become a more effective parent or teacher, list your total score for each of the six components below:

        I. Have a philosophy of discipline   _____
       II. Specify the rules   _____
      III. Be positive   _____
       IV. If punishment is necessary, be fair   _____
        V. Be consistent   _____
       VI. Be a good model   _____

Choose the component with the lowest score and work toward improvement in that area. Reread the component and make a list of specific resolutions for this area for the next week, being sure to choose things that are realistic. At the end of the week look at the list and assess the progress made. If success is evident, add a few additional activities to increase effectiveness in this area, or go onto another area that needs improvement. If success is not evident, revise the original list, deleting and reducing unrealistic resolutions. Continue trying to improve each week by listing changes that should be made in your behavior, and matching the list. Follow this process until you are satisfied with the improvement.

Making and following the discipline improvement plan described will assist parents and teachers in their own self-discipline. This would be another good model to provide for children.

Parents, What is Your "Discipline Quotient?"

	Yes	No
1. Do you have a philosophy about the discipline of your children?	___	___
2. If your spouse asked you about your overall approach to behavior management, cold you describe it?	___	___
3. Have you and your spouse ever discussed your approach to behavior management?	___	___
4. When your child comes home from school, does she or he know exactly what he or she is supposed to do?	___	___
5. Do you specify how you expect your child to behave before she or he has to do so?	___	___
6. Have you established a set of rules you expect your child to follow?	___	___
7. Do you give your child "warm fuzzies" (hugs, smiles, praise, etc.) every day?	___	___
8. Do you praise your child when she or he accomplishes a difficult task?	___	___
9. Do you catch your child being good?	___	___
10. Do you hold your temper when you reprimand your child?	___	___
11. If you take television privileges away from your child, do you give him or her an opportunity to earn them back?	___	___
12. Do you ignore minor disruptions?	___	___
13. If you have more than one child, do you expect them all to follow equivalent rules?	___	___
14. When your child misbehaves, does your response remain about the same from day to day?	___	___
15. When your child does his or her chores, does your response remain about the same?	___	___
16. Do you behave toward your children the way you expect them to behave toward others?	___	___

Teacher, What is Your "Discipline Quotient?"

	Yes	No
1. Do you have a philosophy about discipline in your classroom?	____	____
2. If another teacher asked you about your overall approach to behavior management, could you describe it?	____	____
3. Have you and your colleagues ever discussed your approaches to behavior management?	____	____
4. When your students enter your classroom, do they know exactly what they are supposed to do?	____	____
5. Do you show your students how to behave before they have to do so?	____	____
6. Have you established a set of rules you expect your students to follow?	____	____
7. Do you give each of your students a "warm fuzzie" (hug, smile, praise, etc.) every day?	____	____
8. Do you praise your students when they accomplish a difficult task?	____	____
9. Do you catch your students being good?	____	____
10. Do you hold your temper when you reprimand your students?	____	____
11. If you take recess away from a student, do you provide an opportunity to earn it back?	____	____
12. Do you ignore minor disruptions?	____	____
13. Do you expect all the students to follow the same rules?	____	____
14. When a student misbehaves, does your response remain about he same from day to day?	____	____
15. Do you discipline the girls in your classroom the same way you discipline the boys?	____	____
16. Do you behave towards your students the way you expect them to behave toward each other?	____	____

CHAPTER III

THE SCHOOL ROUTINE

INTRODUCTION

A ROUTINE is any activity which occurs regularly almost as if by habit. There are many activities in schools which occur on a regular basis and it is to the advantage of parents and teachers to be aware of their specific responsibilities in these routines so that cooperative effort can be maximized.

Probably the most common school routine which involves both parents and teachers is homework. Teachers wonder when to assign it and how much to assign. Parents worry about how much they should help their children and how to motivate them to do the homework. The first two articles in this chapter, "Homework from the Parent's Perspective" and "Homework from the Teacher's Perspective," discuss this important part of the school routine.

An area that is usually of great concern to parents and is a source of difficulty for teachers is that of grading and reporting progress. The third article, "Grading and Reporting Progress," discusses what types of information can be effectively communicated by teachers and gleaned by parents from grades and what can be done as a result of reported progress or the lack of it.

Sometimes teachers are fortunate enough to have parents agree to volunteer as tutors. When this occurs it can either be a very rewarding experience for both the teacher and parent volunteer, or it can be a disaster. The recommendations given in the fourth article, "Parents as Classroom Volunteers," will assist parents and teachers in making school volunteering a rewarding an fulfilling experience.

Some students may need extra help. This assistance may be provided by a parent volunteer, another student (peer tutor), or a professional tutor hired by the parents. When a tutor is needed, the suggestions in the article, "When a Child Needs Tutoring," will be beneficial to teacher and parents.

There is usually much discussion and concern among parents and teachers about the curriculum in a school. An aspect of the curriculum which is not obvious is discussed in "The Hidden Curriculum."

The last article in the chapter discusses teachable moments. In "Teachable Moments," parents and teachers are given hints about how they can capitalize on children's varying experiences and activities and cause these to result in meaningful learning experiences.

HOMEWORK FROM THE TEACHER'S PERSPECTIVE

Homework? Both parents and teachers have questions about it! In this article concerns about homework from a teacher's perspective will be addressed. In the next article, suggestions about homework for parents will be provided.

About Homework, teachers ask:

Should I assign it?
Will it help my students?
How much should I assign?

To what degree should parents be involved?

Opinions about homework differ, the research on it is limited, and the research that exists yields inconclusive results. Educators agree that if homework is assigned, it should be for the purposes of (1) reinforcing what has been taught in class and (2) teaching a student independent work skills and responsibility.

To experience success with homework, the teacher should establish a systematic homework procedure and follow it. The procedure should include how and when homework will be assigned, due dates, how feedback will be provided to students and parents, and the consequences for completing and for not completing homework. The teacher should discuss and/or provide written guidelines about homework for students and parents. The guidelines for parents should specify recommendations about parent involvement in the completion of homework.

The type and amount of homework will vary depending on grade level and individual student capabilities. As students progress through school, they should become more independent in their studies. Homework assignments should reflect this growing realization of responsibility and independence. When assigning homework, teachers should take into consideration the skills and ability of the individual student. The type and amount of homework should be varied so that unrealistic demands are not placed on students; yet, all students should be challenged.

Homework should never be assigned as busy-work or punishment. Assignments should be made to reinforce what has been instructed in class. The teacher should explain the purpose of the assignment, review it, and answer any questions to make sure students understand what is to be done.

Interest in homework can be increased by changing the types of assignments. Homework may include reports on television programs, summaries of current events, long-term projects on countries or student hobbies, oral drill exercises, written and oral reports on books, or the making of models to illustrate what has been studied. Students should be encouraged to use their creativity and imagination when completing homework assignments.

The use of home-school contracts is recommended when specific problems arise with homework completion. Guidelines for implementing home-school contracts are specified in Chapter II. Through contractual agreements, cooperative efforts between parents and teachers will help ensure successful homework experiences for children.

HOMEWORK FROM THE PARENT'S PERSPECTIVE

About homework, parents ask:

How can I motivate my child to do homework?
How do I set priorities between homework and outside activities?
How involved should I get with my child's homework?

Parents can help make homework a worthwhile and valuable experience for their child by expressing interest and support for the work and projects that their child brings home. To provide support, parents can offer to supply the resources and materials necessary for completing a homework assignment or to help the child by questioning and listening, but parents should **never** do homework for their child.

Parents can encourage their child to complete homework assignments by providing a quiet, well-lighted study place and schedule a time for homework completion. This scheduled time will vary from student to student and family to family. Parents can provide further encouragement by specifying consequences for completion and non-completion of homework. For example, if all homework is completed, the child will be allowed to watch a favorite television program; otherwise, the homework will be completed during the time of this television program.

In most cases the completion of homework should take precedence over outside activities. However, instances will arise when homework cannot be completed. The parent should determine when a circumstance prevents the completion of homework and inform the teacher in writing of the problem.

If the student is having difficulty with homework completion because of the amount of difficulty, the parent should report this to the teacher. The parent should not demand adjustments in homework assignments, but describe the problem and request suggestions for solving the problem. With homework as with all concerns about students, the best solutions result from a cooperative effort between the parent and teacher.

GRADING AND REPORTING PROGRESS

In an attempt to communicate with parents about student progress, teachers complete Report Cards or Progress Reports. These reports are sent home on a regular basis, usually every six to ten weeks. Two questions can be asked about the intent of these reports. What exactly is the teacher attempting to communicate? How can the parent meaningfully interpret the information in the report?

Because of the very nature of the report card, the information included is very broad and general, and is intended to convey an estimate of student progress in the various curricular areas. If letter grades of A, B, etc., are included on the report card, so should explanations of those letter grades. For example, "A" might mean "excellent" and "B" "very good." If numerical grades are included there should be a similar type of explanation. These numerical grades are usually the student's average in the course.

By reviewing most report cards, parents cannot determine exactly what their child has learned during the course of the grading period. They can, however, get a general idea of how much progress, in the teacher's opinion, has been made. If the grade can be interpreted as "good" or "very good," then parents can conclude that their child is doing well in school.

If, however, the grade can be interpreted as "in need of improvement" parents should be alert to the fact that their child is not doing well in school. Parents should use the grade as a signal that something needs to be done to improve their child's performance in school.

What can be done? The first thing to do is to contact the teacher and set up a meeting. Because the teacher has maintained records that have lead to a final grade, she should be able to identify problem areas and suggest ways to remediate the problems.

By working together, parents and teachers should be able to improve each student's progress. This improvement is a responsibility that is shared by the teacher, the parents and the student. By working in concert, progress can be made.

PARENTS AS VOLUNTEERS

Teachers regularly find themselves in the precarious position of having too much to do, and too little time to do it in. Their primary responsibilities are to ensure that students are progressing in the curriculum and gaining necessary academic skills. To achieve this goal, teachers must plan for and instruct students, organize the curriculum, learning resources and the environment, establish schedules and a classroom management system, conference with parents, keep records and report student progress, and deal with discipline and other student problems. These activities are conducted for all students in a classroom of children with numerous socioeconomic, academic, and cultural backgrounds; yet the teacher must attempt to plan for and motivate each one.

If instructing students were the only responsibility of teachers, it would be a difficult job, requiring great skill. There are, however, many other duties of a non-academic nature that are required of teacher. Additional tasks that teachers must complete include among others, keeping attendance records, attending meetings, collecting lunch money, supervising in the lunchroom and on the playground, and monitoring students in the halls.

One solution to the teacher's problem of having too much to do and too little time to do it is for parents to volunteer as aides in the teacher's classroom. The parent-teacher team is a viable means of providing an optimal education environment for the students.

When parents volunteer to work as aides in a school, several guidelines should be followed. First, careful thought should be given to the effects the parent's presence might have on his/her child. If it is suspected that the child would be more comfortable if the parent were in another classroom, this should be of primary consideration.

Second, parents and teachers must also work closely together to decide exactly what the parent's duties should be. Before reaching this decision the parent should observe the teacher's routines, procedures, and discipline techniques long enough to know what s/he would be comfortable doing. Once this decision is made, the parents' duties should be specified and written down so there can be no questions about what the parent is to do.

Third, open lines of commumnication must be established and maintained. This is essential for the effective functioning of the team.

Words of caution are also in order for the team members as they begin the school year. The teacher must maintain leadership in the team because of her professional responsibilities in the school. Also, the teacher should not expect a parent to solve problems in the classroom that she can not solve. Finally, the parent must be able to honor her commitment to the teacher and the students. Many people must rely on the parent's prompt and regular arrival.

If these few guidelines are followed, and the warnings heeded, a parent-teacher team can go a long way to solving every teacher's problem of always having too few hours in the day.

WHEN A CHILD NEEDS TUTORING

As the school year progresses, it is likely that some students in every classroom will need extra help in specific areas. One solution to this problem is to use "peer tutors" in the classroom or at home.

A peer tutor is another student who is about the same age as the student who needs extra help. Most often a teacher will choose as a peer tutor a student who is academically quite advanced. Another, and perhaps better, choice would be a student who knows just a little bit more than the child who is in need of tutoring. This way both students are improving their mastery of the academic skills.

The tutoring might take place during school hours or after school, whichever is most convenient. However, a student should not be deprived of recess, art, music, physical education, or the like in order to receive the tutoring. When this is done, the child might resent missing an enjoyable activity and think of the tutoring as a form of punishment.

Whoever is chosen as a tutor, and whenever it is done, adult supervision is always necessary. The teacher or parent should tell the tutor exactly what to do and how to do it. Without this supervision, more harm than good can be done.

Another solution to the problem of academic problems is for parents to hire a professional tutor for their child, or to take advantage of community tutoring services. To find a tutor, a parent might call his/her child's school, the school district administrative offices, or a community "hot line." Local YMCA's might have after school tutoring services, as might local community education programs. Teachers who also tutor children often advertise in the classified pages of the local papers, and professional tutoring services are often listed in the yellow pages under "Tutoring."

When parents choose a tutor for their child they should try to get someone who is professionally qualified to serve as a tutor. It should also be expected that the tutor stay in close contact with the child's teacher, and provide frequent reports on the child's progress.

Parents and teachers should not wait until an academic problem becomes insurmountable before providing extra help for students. Delay can turn even a mild problem into a severe one.

THE HIDDEN CURRICULUM

When asked about his school, a principal stated, "Our adopted curriculum is sequenced, grade-level appropriate, and followed by most of the teachers; however, I am very concerned about our 'hidden curriculum.' " Because "hidden curriculum" was not readily understood, the principal explained that what he and his teachers taught children and planned to teach them (the adopted curriculum was straightforward. It was what they taught children when they were not intending to teach them at all (the hidden curriculum) that worried him.

Actually the principal was using "hidden curriculum" to refer to the concept of "modeling," a social learning term which means that children learn by watching another person's behavior and the consequences of the behavior. Experimental results have proven that a child copies behaviors more completely when the model is perceived as significant, powerful, in control, and similar to the child. Who fits this description for effective models more than parents and teachers?

Additionally, research studies have shown that children model appropriate and positive behaviors as well as inappropriate and negative behaviors. Parents and teachers should examine their behaviors to determine what they are teaching their children via the "hidden curriculum."

One good example of the modeling of inappropriate behavior is when two children are fighting and they are spanked for fighting. By his or her actions, the adult in this situation is saying, "you are not to solve your problems by hitting, but I solve my problems by hitting." Another example of adults not practicing what they preach is when children are loud and rowdy, and the adult intervenes by yelling. Examples such as these are numerous—expecting children to read but not reading; asking children to be on time, but not being on time; warning children about drug abuse, yet drinking alcohol, smoking cigarettes, and taking double-strength tablets for headaches.

The behaviors of parents and teachers are a powerful influence on the behaviors of children, and the ultimate result is that for the most part teachers teach the way they were taught and parents parent the way they were parented. What is your "hidden curriculum" teaching children about effective teaching and effective parenting? What behaviors are you modeling for your children?

TEACHABLE MOMENTS

Parents are teachers of their children whether they want to be or not. Both parents as teachers and the professional teacher must realize that circumstances result in what is called a "teachable moment." This is a time when something happens to spur the child's interest and she/he wants further information. The optimal time for learning is at the very moment when interest is highest.

There are many examples of teachable moments in the home setting. When a parent and child are making a cake and the child says, "I wonder why vanilla is black." When a child sees a particular type of structure and asks, "Why is that bigger at the bottom?" If the parent fails to follow with responses to the child's interest in the subject, the opportunity for the child to learn when motivation is at its peak is lost.

Teachable moments occur in school as well as at home. It is the wise and flexible teacher who is able to optimally utilize these specific times. The teacher may have prepared extensive lecture and activities about state government when a student states concern about a proposal before County Council. The effective teacher will discuss the issue and then attempt to relate it to the presentation about state government. The best mathematics instruction occurs during times when students are attempting to apply skills such as trying to decide what admission to charge for a dance in order to make a profit or how to attractively and efficiently utilize space and design a page for the school newspaper.

An important characteristic of effective teaching is the ability to use circumstances to teach children responsibility because the goal of all teachers, whether in school or at home, is the creation of independent, self-sufficient adults. Children must begin early to assume responsibility for their own behaviors and to do things for themselves. Although it is easier to make the child's bed, fix the sandwiches, brush the hair, organize the work-folder, copy the assignments, etc., doing it together and eventually having the child do it, will result in the child gaining the skill. Helping the child solve academic and social problems rather than solving them will result in the development of problem solving abilities and independent thinking.

Taking advantage of and even creating "teachable moments" results in more effective teaching and learning. Teachers and parents will encourage more independent thinking and problem solving in their children as they become better able to capitalize on "teachable moments."

CHAPTER IV

SPECIAL CHILDREN AND PROBLEMS

INTRODUCTION

IT IS MORE important that parents and teachers work cooperatively when a specific difficulty has been identified than at any other time. When children are in need of special education both parents and teachers should understand the services which are available and the roles and responsibilities of the specialized personnel. It is when parents and teachers understand the special programs and work cooperatively with the other specialized professionals on the educational team that special education services for children are maximally beneficial. The first two articles in this chapter, "What is Special Education?" and "Utilizing Special Personnel in Schools," explain special education and how parents and teachers can effectively utilize the services of specialized professionals.

Some of the special problems which students may experience are stress, learning disabilities, school phobia or avoidance, and attention deficit disorder. These problems are defined and discussed in the chapter and possible interventions are proposed.

A group of children which can be challenging yet sometimes propose problems for parents and teachers are the gifted and talented children and youth. The characteristics of these children and suggestions for challenging them are in the final article in the chapter, "The Gifted and Talented: A Challenge for Parents and Teachers."

WHAT IS SPECIAL EDUCATION?

In 1975, federal legislation was passed that mandated that an appropriate education be made available to all handicapped students of school age (Public Law 94-142). Up until that time, a school district could arbitrarily exclude handicapped children, and many did. When the legislation was implemented, there was a significant increase in the number of handicapped children being educated in our schools, and a parallel increase in the number of special education teachers.

Students who are handicapped fall into one or more of the following categories: emotionally handicapped, learning disabled, mentally handicapped, visually handicapped, hearing handicapped, speech impaired or physically handicapped. Although these labels imply that they identify students with common characteristics, it is not necessarily so. All but the most severely handicapped students are more like their normal peers than unlike them. Within each category there are also levels. Students can be mildly, moderately, or severely handicapped.

Students are generally referred for special education services by their regular classroom teachers when it is suspected that a student's needs cannot be met without additional help. A student's strengths and weaknesses are identified through a thorough evaluation procedure, and based on that evaluation, a decision is made about placement in a resource room or self-contained special education classroom.

Resource rooms are designed to meet the needs of children who have mild learning problems and who could benefit from special instruction designed to meet their individual needs. Students assigned to a resource room are given the unique opportunity to work individually or in small groups with a specially trained teacher for short periods each day. The teacher develops each child's instruction to eliminate learning problems. When this goal is met, the student no longer attends class in the resource room. If it is realized that the child's needs are not being met in the resource program, she or he may be recommended for a self-contained program.

Students who are assigned to a self-contained special education classroom have moderate to severe learning problems. It is felt that these students could benefit from more intense special instruction. In self-contained classrooms the specially trained teachers design individual instruction that builds on each child's strengths in an attempt to improve areas of academic and social weaknesses. Students who are assigned to a self-contained classroom can be returned to a regular classroom when their academic and social skills would ensure their success.

Many parents and educators question the need for assigning a child a specific label in order for that child to receive special education services. The most often used rationale is that labeling is necessary for funding purposes. However, there are states which provide special services without labeling their students (California, Massachusetts, South Dakota).

All school districts offer some types of special education programs and 10 to 15% of the school-aged population will qualify and benefit from these services. When a child is in need of special education, it is most important that all persons involved with the child's education (parents, special teachers, classroom teachers, speech clinicians, guidance counselors, etc.) work together in order to plan and implement a coordinated and complementary program.

UTILIZING SPECIAL PERSONNEL IN SCHOOLS

Schools are much different today than they were a number of years ago when school personnel typically consisted of the teachers, principal, and librarian. In the schools of the 1980's, parents and teachers have a variety of specialized personnel who can assist with the education, management, and development of their children. Some of the specialists in schools are school psychologists, counselors, speech clinicians, resource teachers, and remedial teachers. Unfortunately, parents and teachers sometimes do not understand the roles and responsibilities of these specialized professionals and, consequently, do not effectively utilize their services. The purpose of this article is to briefly describe some of the services which are available to parents, teachers, and students.

The school psychologist is a professional who must be certified and sometimes is licensed. This person has received specialized training in the administration and interpretation of psychological and educational tests and in specialized interventions with children. Usually a school psychologist will serve more than one school and may have limited time in any one school. The school psychologist's job description may include a variety of responsibilities, and these are specified by the school district in which the psychologist is employed. Typically the school psychologist's primary responsibility is the evaluation of children who have been referred to be considered for placement in a special education program. Other activities include developing inservice programs for teachers and parents, designing individual intervention programs for students, and consulting with parents and teachers.

Most schools have a guidance counselor. The counselors have had teaching experience and are certified by the State Department of Education. The functioning of the counselor depends on the school district and level of school. In the middle and high schools, counselors often advise and schedule students. This responsibility is very time consuming. At the elementary school level counselors establish groups for children who have particular problems. Examples of these groups are those for children of divorced parents or for shy and withdrawn children. Counselors also provide individual counseling to students with specialized problems, consult with classroom teachers about effective ways to work with particular children and problems, and instruct entire classes about particular subjects such as how to avoid abuse.

The speech therapist or clinician works with children who have particular speech problems or may be language delayed. This professional must be certified and may be licensed. Usually, a clinician is responsible for students in more than one school. Speech clinicians work with students who have an articulation problem or other speech disorders and those whose receptive and/or expressive language has not developed at the appropriate rate. Speech clinicians work with students individually and in groups. Speech clinicians are involved in screening children to determine those in need of therapy, evaluating to determine specific needs, and then implementing programs which will meet the individual needs of children.

Resource teachers are certified in one or more areas of special education (learning disabilities, emotionally handicapped, or mental retardation) and work with those students who are experiencing special academic or social difficulty. Resource teachers usually work with students in small groups and see each child for one or two periods each day. For a student to be placed in the resource program, the regular classroom teacher refers the child for psycho-educational testing, the parents must sign permission for the evaluation, the school psychologist assesses the ability and academic achievement of the student, and a group of professionals along with the parents meet to decide the specific needs of the child. At this meeting an individual educational program is developed (IEP). The IEP specifies the specific objectives for the child and the specialized methods and materials recommended in order to reach the objectives.

Most schools have remedial or compensatory teachers. These teachers instruct students whose scores on a group standardized test indicate that they are significantly below their peers. Usually, these students are in the lower 25% of their class in a particular subject. Remedial teachers in mathematics and/or reading instruct those students who qualify as needing assistance. The instruction is typically conducted in small groups with specialized materials and equipment.

The descriptions of special professionals in schools is very brief and designed to provide teachers and parents with an overview of those services which are available. Whenever an individual child is considered for any special service, the teacher typically is the person who makes the referral or suggestion, and the parent is involved in making the decision about appropriate utilization of services and must ultimately grant permission for the program. Thus, it is most important that parents and teachers understand specialized services and personnel which are available. Parents and teachers should feel comfortable asking questions of any specialized school professional about the services provided and how to obtain the services so that better understanding and utilization of these professionals will result.

CHILDREN AND STRESS

When we think about stress we do not usually think in terms of children. We have an image in our society of childhood as a happy carefree time. This view shows that as adults we have forgotten the difficulties of childhood. No period of life is free from stress, and childhood is a time when we are very susceptible to stress. The pains, fears, and worries of children are very real and often more deeply felt and less readily forgotten than those of adults who have developed greater coping skills and have wider social supports. In this article, we will discuss children and stress: what it is, how it affects the health of children, what creates stress for children, why some children are more vulnerable to stress than others, and how adults can help children cope with stress.

Whether in children or in adults stress is the same process. Stress results whenever any event demands readjustment in the child's ways of dealing with the world. Internally, stress is basically a state of nervous system arousal. When faced with stress, our bodies get into a generalized state of preparedness for action, sometimes called the "fight or flight response." Our hearts beat faster, blood pressure rises, blood vessels to the heart dilate, more blood is directed to skeletal muscles, pupils of the eyes widen, etc.

The fight or flight response can damage the body's health in at least two different ways. First, it may be direct damage to the tissues...especially those of the circulatory system. Elevated blood pressure places strain on the heart, kidneys and blood vessels. This strain may result in ruptures of weaker parts of the system and may cause microscopic tears in the walls of arteries. Second, and more important to the health of children, the response may suppress the body's natural defenses against disease. The adrenal hormones associated with the fight or flight response naturally suppress the whole immune system.

A number of studies have examined the association between stress and illness in children. One researcher found that one-fourth of all children's sore throats followed a family crisis. Another studied the utilization of health services by young children and found that children were twice as likely to experience illness on a day when some stressful episode had occurred such as a family fight or job tensions.

Children are exposed to a wide variety of stressors. We will discuss a few of the most potent which affect large numbers of children.

1. Changes in the Environment

When children must adjust to new situations or environments, stress often results. Examples of changes in environment include moving to a new city, state, or neighborhood, changing schools, or entering school.

2. Disruptions in Primary Relationships

Children are often under stress when there is a birth of a sibling. Additionally, many children must adjust to the separation and/or divorce of their parents. Sometimes a death in the family will occur or the child or a member of his or her family may have a serious illness requiring hospitalization.

3. Developmental Changes

There are many developmental changes with which children must cope. Often these cause stress. Some of the changes are physiological, cognitive, social, and academic.

Unfortunately, many children unsuccessfully cope with stress. These are the children with schizoid or sociopathic behaviors, nervous habits or tics, and sexual misconduct; or the ones who attempt suicide, sell and use drugs, run away, or maliciously injure others and/or property.

Why do some children develop health problems in response to stressors with which most of their peers are able to cope? Why is one child unable to cope successfully with a new sibling or with beginning school when most children are able to cope? There is no single, simple answer to these questions but a number of factors should be considered.

A major part of the answer is that not all children entering school or facing some other such common stressor have had the same recent history of stress. Some have faced no other major stressors in the same period. The effects of stressors seem to be additive, perhaps even multiplicative. Children need to rest their adjustment abilities for a while after coping with a stressor. The greater the stress the more time needed for recuperation. When stress crowds upon stress depriving the child of necessary recuperation time, the damage which may be done is greatly increased.

The extent to which children possess skills for coping with stress varies greatly. Some children have great difficulty asking for help. Some find it hard to express their feelings openly. Others cannot resist peer pressure or adult demands which are unrealisitic. Children lacking such social skills will be more vulnerable to stress.

Children are less vulnerable to stress when there are many people they can call on for help and support. For the very young child the family is the only available source of social support. As the child grows older the potential sources of support multiply. Adults such as neighbors and teachers become possible sources of support. Even more vital is the support which may be given by peers. All children, however, do not have equal opportunity for such support; isolation, prejudice, and language barriers may restrict a child's opportunities for support. And all children do not equally take advantage of the opportunities for social support which come their way. When poor communication exists between the parent and the child, especially if there are no other adults available as alternate sources of support, the child is highly vulnerable to stress.

A personality pattern, sometimes known as coronary prone behavior or as Type A behavior has been described in adults. This pattern is characterized by competitiveness, a sense of time urgency, and higher than average levels of aggression and hostility. There is now evidence that Type A behavior can be identified in children. Unfortunately, there are many forces in our society which tend to mold Type A behavior in children. In our schools, for instance, time urgency is reinforced, promptness is rewarded, finishing work first is rewarded, and competitiveness is encouraged.

There are a variety of ways that we can help children cope with stress. One important consideration is effective communication. Children, just like adults, need someone who will listen empathetically and will respect their problem-solving ability. They need someone who will not ignore or belittle their feelings. They don't need someone who will offer empty reassurances, unsolicited advice or pat solutions. Unfortunately, this sort of listener is hard for an adult to find; for a child it is often nearly impossible. The child under stress who lacks a pattern of communication must search for a listener who is trustworthy and must spend time building the bridges of open communication before the feelings of stress, fear, and anguish can be dealt with. Too often the trustworthy listener cannot be found in time.

Parents need to understand normal child growth and development in order to have realistic goals and expectations for their children. Unrealistic goals and expectations can become a source of stress for children. Understanding normal child growth and development allows parents to recognize that the child may need time out to cope. It also permits them to recognize when the child truly is failing to develop normally and to mobilize appropriate resources to cope with whatever problem is presenting itself.

Children should be involved in planning and preparing for the predictable stressors. School, a new sibling, a new home, a stay in the hospital, all are less threatening if the child knows what to expect and especially if the child has been a party to making plans for the event.

Children can be taught skills in problem solving. Such skills as identifying feelings, recognizing cause and effect, understanding consequences, identifying and weighing alternatives, and evaluating probable outcomes can be taught to children. Perhaps we spend too much time teaching children what they should do and too little time teaching them how to decide for themselves.

Stress is an inescapable part of human life. Children can suffer from the effects of too much stress that is poorly coped with. But successful coping with stress is growth promoting...it is essential for wellness. Children can better learn to cope with stress if they have adults with which they can successfully communicate, who provide a support system, and assist the child in acquiring appropriate social skills.

IDENTIFYING LEARNING DISABILITIES

What is a learning disability? A child is said to have a learning disability if he or she is not making the academic gains that are expected based on the child's age, grade placement, and intelligence. This lack of achievement may be evident in any of the following academic areas: basic reading skill, reading comprehension, math calculation, math reasoning, oral expression, written expression, or listening comprehension. The discrepancy between ability and achievement must be great enough to warrant special assistance from someone other than the regular classroom teacher. Usually it is a special education teacher who attempts to improve the child's achievement so that the discrepancy is reduced or eliminated.

The theoretical causes of learning disabilities are many and varied: developmental lag, neurological dysfunction, teaching failure, and lack of motivation are a few of the most prevalent theories. Some theorists contend that the cause must be identified, whereas others contend that the cause is not nearly as important as what is done to alleviate the problem.

When a teacher or parent suspects that a child has a learning disability, the child should be referred for a series of tests used to identify children who might benefit from special education placement. The principal of each school should know the procedures to follow.

It is important that parents and teachers work together to determine if a child has a learning disability. Both have information that may help in the testing process and both should be actively involved in designing an educational program that will enable the child to make the most of his or her abilities.

UNDERSTANDING AND MANAGING CHILDREN WITH ATTENTION DEFICIT DISORDER

The accurate diagnosis and successful treatment of attention deficit disorder (ADD) requires coordination and communication among physicians, teachers, psychologists, and parents. ADD is characterized as occurring with or without hyperactivity and is up to 10 times more frequent in boys than girls. There is some evidence that it may be inherited. Longitudinal studies are revealing that individuals with ADD exhibit characteristics into adulthood.

ADD exists when a child displays, for his or her mental and chronological age, signs of developmentally inappropriate inattention, impulsivity and in some cases hyperactivity. These signs are usually reported by adults in the child's environment such as the child's parents and teachers. Symptoms typically worsen in situations that require self-application as in the classroom. Symptoms may be less visible in a one-to-one situation.

Diagnosis should be based on a combination of medical, psychological, and educational findings. Characteristics to be considered in the diagnostic process include:

1. Chronic inattention and distractibility identified at an early age that has persisted over time.
2. Behavior problems that are not due to specific situations; environment is not the sole cause of the problem.
3. Significant problems of attention and concentration as indicated by observation and testing.
4. Overactivity and/or impulsivity and distractibility.
5. Lack of mental retardation or emotional disturbance.
6. Lack of conduct and anxiety problems.

Successful treatment depends upon the needs of the individual child. Thus, the prescribed intervention will vary with the diagnosed difficulty and the goals of treatment. A variety of treatments are currently being used independently and in combination. Some of these are pharmacological, behavioral, or nutritional.

environmental, and cognitive. All treatments have reported a positive influence with some children but no treatment has proven completely effective with all children. The most common treatment is a combination of pharmacological with behavioral. Interventions which have proven to be unsuccessful in the treatment of ADD are psychotherapy and typical counseling.

The drugs most commonly prescribed are methylphenidate (ritalin), dextroamphetamine (dexadrine), or pemoline (cylert). Medication often makes the child better able to interact with the academic environment; however, not all children respond to drug treatment. Common side effects of the stimulant medications are insomina and other sleep disturbances, decreased appetite and weight loss, irritability, abdominal pains, drowsiness, headaches, nausea, dizziness, and lethargy.

A behavioral approach for the treatment of ADD includes typical behavior modification programs. Particular behaviors of children that need to be changed are stated very specifically, a measurement of the rate and/or duration of these behaviors is made, and an appropriate and systematic behavioral intervention is planned and implemented in an attempt to change the behavior.

A variety of diets have been recommended in the treatment of ADD. Some of these include eliminating foods with additives and other foods with wheat and sugar. The use of megavitamins has also been suggested. Some research findings indicate that children have a positive reaction to dietary interventions. The most recent study reported that megavitamin therapy is not helpful and may be harmful.

Interventions which have proven successful but are not often utilized include environmental and cognitive. Environmental intervention is changing the child's surroundings in an effort to help the child become less distractible. Examples include putting the child's desk at the front of the row so as to reduce distractions or putting the child next to a file cabinet rather than a book case. Cognitive intervention involves teaching children to verbally instruct themselves and self-monitor their own behavior. To effectively use the cognitive approach, adults must rehearse and role play with children. Children who are able to evaluate their own behaviors and become active participants in their treatment programs have the best results.

A discussion of attention deficit disorder has been ongoing for over a decade; however, research at the present time is not definitive because of difficulties in conducting the research. One of the difficulties is that ADD is a comprehensive diagnosis and children diagnosed may have as many as six different problems. Another concern is that there is little data regarding long-term effects and almost no information related to girls because they constitute such a small percentage of the total ADD population. It is known that effective diagnosis and treatment depend upon the individual child and that the most beneficial treatment is usually a combination of approaches with clear, systematic, and regular communication between physicians, psychologists, parents, teachers, and most importantly the child.

SCHOOL PHOBIA: WHEN A CHILD AVOIDS SCHOOL

School phobia is the phenomenon in which a child experiences marked anxiety and fear related to attending school and subsequently refuses or fails to attend. A phobia is usually caused by unfortunate, unusual and vivid earlier experiences and has been discussed in educational and psychological literature since 1941. More often than not, children who are experiencing school phobia exhibit physical as well as psychological symptoms. These children become physically ill when required to attend school. Common ailments include nausea, backaches, and rashes. The incidence of the syndrome in the school-aged population is reported to be 17 per 1000. Although this disorder has been known for over 40 years and occurs in almost every school, it is often misunderstood and mistreated by parents and teachers.

School phobics may be boys or girls of any age; however, most often school phobics are boys who are from 10 to 12 years and of above average intellectual ability. The syndrome is equally distributed among social classes and is not influenced by the birth order or position of the child in the family. It is just as prevalent for eldest, middle or youngest children.

Effective treatment of school phobia requires close cooperation between the home and school. Most phobic reactions require the intervention of a therapist or counselor as well as school personnel and the family. Successful treatment is characterized by the use of a variety of approaches and considerations.

The most common and reportedly most successful approach for treating school phobia is systematic desensitization. With this approach, the child is gradually exposed to the school environment. Initially, the child is encouraged to talk about school, then visit the school when no other students or teachers are there, go for a short period of time, and gradually increase the time in school each day. This process occurs over the course of several weeks. While the child is being exposed to the school environment for longer and longer periods, he is taught relaxation exercises to use in order to become more comfortable in school.

More often than not, the school phobic child has the concurrent fear of leaving home. Thus, in addition to helping the child become more comfortable in the school environment, it is often necessary to reestablish the proper parent-child hierarchy and strengthen the sibling subsystem within the family.

The successful treatment of school phobia always involves the establishment of a support system for the child at school. The student must feel there is someone and some place where he can go to relax when he becomes anxious and fearful.

There are many fears and anxieties which interfere with the productive functioning of children and adults. One which is often misunderstood in children is that of attending school. Helping children overcome this fear is tedious and trying for parents and teachers; however, the syndrome can be successfully treated. Effective treatment requires cooperation between home and school, patience and persistence, and usually the involvement of a therapist or counselor.

THE GIFTED AND TALENTED: A CHALLENGE FOR PARENTS AND TEACHERS

One group of exceptional children currently receiving much attention is the gifted and talented. It is fortunate that these precocious children are finally being recognized because they have not been provided necessary services and programs for a number of years. In order to meet the challenge of educating these special youngsters we must learn who they are, what programs are available, what happens to them when they become adults, and the responsibilities of parents and teachers.

Who are the gifted and talented? Definitions vary from school district to school district and state to state. The US Office of Education has defined gifted children as those "who by nature of outstanding abilities are capable of high performance." These outstanding abilities might be displayed in any one or all of six categories: general intellectual ability, specific academic aptitude, leadership ability, ability in the visual or performing arts, creative thinking or psychomotor ability. The most current definition states, "gifted and talented students are those who are identified in grades 1-12 as possessing demonstrated or potential abilities for high performance in academic or artistic areas and therefore require services or programs not ordinarily provided by the regular school program."

What are the best ways to challenge intellectually gifted students so that they don't waste their school years? There are a number of different programs and much controversy about which of these is best for the gifted. One approach is acceleration by skipping grades or levels or condensing several years' work into one. The idea of acceleration is built into many public and private schools that offer Advance Placement courses—which are honored as fulfilling the introductory level course in a college curriculum. Another approach is segregating or tracking the gifted, clustering these ablest students in special classes if only for a part of each day. A third approach is enrichment which means any number of things from independent projects to clubs to extra courses. Many programs for the gifted go beyond academics and encourage exceptional creativity, physical ability and leadership.

Some programs are sponsored by universities with special interest in gifted children. One such program was launched at Duke University and is a talent search to identify academically superior seventh grade youngsters by using math and verbal Scholastic Aptitude Test scores. Students who qualify are provided academic summer camp in the form of rigorous, advanced courses.

Many parents who are dissatisfied with public school programs for the gifted have been enrolling their youngsters in private schools. It is true that private schools can be less well-equipped in terms of sports, science and media facilities; however, the smaller classes and more intimate exchange of a private school make it less likely that a really gifted child will be overlooked or allowed to tune out.

Parental assertiveness and curiosity are also creating a demand for new services such as the **Gifted Children Newsletter.** Its purpose is to translate the lastest from academia into "lay language" for parents. This publication touches on everything from using grandparents as mentors to fundraising ideas to drawing that fine line between nurturing true brilliance and pressuring "pseudo-giftedness."

Do exceptionally bright youngsters turn out healthy, wealthy, and wise, or just neurotic? Happily, the old myth that gifted children are in for a life of misery has been dispelled by one of the few studies of any weight done on these promising youngsters. The Terman Study, a lifelong, ongoing follow-up of 1,528 California children with IQ's over 135 was begun by Lewis B. Terman in 1921. Nine hundred of the original subjects are still alive and involved in the study. According to the study results, exceptional intelligence does not impede achieving personal happiness and success.

What should parents and teachers provide for gifted children? They should make sure the children receive the best education possible, involving them in extracurricular programs, and not overemphasizing school work. Balance is essential for these children with the velcro minds where everything sticks. Because everything sticks these children are far ahead in cognitive skills and various talents; nevertheless, they are still youngsters, and they deserve the right to be children.

CHAPTER V

OTHER TOPICS OF MUTUAL CONCERN

INTRODUCTION

THERE ARE NUMEROUS topics which do not fit any particular category but are of mutual importance to parents and teachers. Many of these involve current research and recent approaches to improving learning and behavior. A topic which should be of particular concern to parents and teachers is nutrition. There are many current findings regarding the relationship between diet and behavior, and some of these are discussed in the first article, "The Link Between Nutrition and Behavior."

Teachers and parents have hectic schedules and numerous tasks to complete. Thus, the second article, "Time Management: When You Have Too Much To Do and Too Little Time," will be beneficial in helping make better use of a valuable resource—time.

Microcomputers have become very prevalent in schools. More often than not children know more about the machines than either parents or teachers. The article, "Computers in Education: The Present, The Possibilities, The Problems," is designed to provide parents and teachers with necessary background information regarding the use of microcomputers in schools.

Much research and learning is occurring in the area of brain functioning and how to maximize use of our most valuable organ—the brain. Two articles, "Recognizing a Child's Learning Style" and

"The Bifunctional Brain in the Classroom," discuss how parents and teachers can use their research to benefit children.

The final article, "A Productive Summer Vacation," discusses what parents and teachers can do to make summer a valuable time. The implementation of the suggested recommendations for community and family activities can result in a vacation which is not only full of fun but full of exciting and rewarding learning experiences as well.

THE LINK BETWEEN NUTRITION
AND BEHAVIOR

As the evidence for a link between what people eat and how they behave increases, more and more adults are paying close attention to their family's eating habits. What people eat, what they do not eat, and how often they eat can all affect how they behave and how they feel. This is as true for adults as it is for children.

Some people are sensitive to certain foods, and because of these sensitivities, their moods and behaviors might be affected. Some of the more common problem foods are sugar, yeast, and chocolate. Nutrients in some foods can create chemical imbalances in certain people. Conversely, too little of specific nutrients found in certain foods can create chemical imbalances. Vitamin deficiencies have also been implicated. For example, too little Vitamin C can be responsible for sudden changes in mood.

The effects food can have on people are varied. Food can cause hypoactivity (too little activity and motion), or it can cause hyperactivity (too much activity and motion). It can affect the ability to concentrate and the ability to remember things. It can cause irritability, depression, fatigue, or insominia. Peoples' reactions are determined by their own physical makeup.

Obviously these reactions can have a real impact on a child's ability to take advantage of the educational situation. For this reason, parents and teachers should be aware of the influence of food on children's behavior. Close observation of children can help these adults determine if there is a possible cause-effect relationship.

One of the things adults should look for is sudden changes in behavior or mood shortly after a child eats something. This sudden change might indicate a food sensitivity. Adults should also watch for distinct changes in activity level, from normal to below normal or above normal. For example, eating something with a high sugar content might result in an initial increase in activity, followed 20 minutes later by irritability or tiredness.

Parents and teachers should help children learn good nutritional habits through instruction and example. This would go far toward balancing the relationship between food and behavior. If there is a suspicion that a severe problem exists, a nutritionist or physician should be consulted to help determine a plan that could improve a child's learning and behavior.

TIME MANAGEMENT: WHEN YOU HAVE TOO MUCH TO DO AND TOO LITTLE TIME

Both parents and teachers have hectic schedules and numerous tasks to complete each day. Teachers manage student behavior, instruct, plan, schedule, communicate with parents and other school personnel, do administrative tasks and paperwork among other things. For parents who combine a career with the responsibilities of managing a home and family, it is no wonder that time is at a premium. For parents who are full time homemakers, it seems that the number of tasks to complete always increases to match the number of hours in the day. Because of their numerous responsibilities, many teachers and parents constantly feel harried and bogged down in a swamp of routine chores and interruptions. This may be because they have not learned to manage their most valuable resource — time.

There are a number of time management techniques that may prove helpful for parents and teachers. The first is to decide what to accomplish, i.e., write goals and then schedule appropriate amounts of time to reach the goals, remembering to establish goals that are reachable considering the amount of available time.

Sometimes parents and teachers have time-consuming tasks to complete and make the mistake of waiting until they can schedule a block of time to complete the entire task. The more productive approach would be to break the task into small units and complete these as time permits. If a teacher has 30 papers to grade, she may have time to grade two of these before the faculty meeting and four more while waiting for the car pool, and 20% of the task is completed. A parent could make the casserole for dinner while preparing breakfast.

Effective time managers use time efficiently, they don't waste time and procrastinate. Everyone should periodically examine their schedules and activities critically to determine procedures for becoming more efficient. Would having labeled cans or baskets for each subject's seatwork keep the teacher and students organized and avoid the sorting of papers at the end of the day? Could 15 minute bathroom breaks be eliminated and the teacher allow each student to go to the bathroom as necessary? Could two or three teachers work together to make learning centers or activities and reduce the preparation time for all? Could parents begin dinner while helping their children organize and complete homework? Could multiplication facts or reading be reviewed in the car on the way to school? Could television time for parents and children be reduced to one hour daily to increase time for accomplishing other tasks?

Other time management suggestions that may be helpful to parents and teachers include:

- Make a "to do" list and check when each task is completed.
- Be aware of your best work time and schedule difficult tasks accordingly.
- Avoid perfection, do the task and go to the next.
- Use waiting time (for meetings, appointments, etc.) effectively.
- Use your commuting time.

Although teachers and parents sometimes complain that they have too much to do and not enough time, they should make time to engage in the activities that they consider most valuable and important. And one of the most valuable is to schedule time for yourself. This special "me" time will make it much more likely that all other time-consuming tasks will be completed.

COMPUTERS IN EDUCATION: THE PRESENT, THE POSSIBILITIES, THE PROBLEMS

Many educators and parents of school-aged children believe that microcomputers have the potential to revolutionize education. This belief and ultimate challenge has resulted in a rush of often undirected activity to obtain microcomputers and to teach teachers to make them an integral part of the curriculum. This surge of microcomputer activity in schools ranges from pre-school to postgraduate. Parents want their children to be computer literate. Teachers must become literate to keep pace with their students.

The Present

Currently, most schools have purchased a single microcomputer and limited software. Usually, the computer is located in the media center or on a cart which is moved from classroom to classroom. Typically, there has been no plan about how the computer will be utilized in the school. Thus, the teachers who use it are those who have microcomputers at home and/or have enough interest to learn to use the school computer.

The interested teachers request the purchase of appropriate software for their curriculum content. Finding appropriate software that coordinates with the curriculum, is motivating, will run, and is easy for students to use independently is difficult; and software is expensive. The expense results in making many administrators reluctant to purchase it. Additionally, much software has not been reviewed by teachers and is not instructionally appropriate.

Even though only a limited number of interested teachers in a school use the computer, there is a scheduling problem. This problem results because of having only one computer, and several teachers who would like to use it. Consequently, the teachers who would like to use the computer for remediation or instruction have access to it only a limited amount of time. Additionally, the scheduling of who will use the computer creates such problems that some interested teachers decide not to bother.

The Possibilities

Hopefully computers will not be just a fad but will become an integral and important part of the educational program. They certainly have the capability to be so. This is not to say that computers will replace teachers. However, they can replace some of the tasks that teachers perform. The microcomputer with appropriate software can drill students, give impersonal feedback about how the students are doing, and systematically record their progress. Additionally, microcomputers could assist teachers in managing the incredible number of records which they are required to maintain. Examples of teacher paperwork including recording attendance, lunch information, progress of students through the curriculum, and students' grades. Thus, the microcomputer could free teachers to work creatively with an ever increasing amount of information and to provide students with problem solving skills to use when approaching new situations and information.

The possibility of microcomputers becoming a tool for use by teachers and students will only become reality if computers are recognized as a viable and crucial part of the educational program just as textbooks, paper, pencils, and blackboards are. For some students and teachers having sufficient computers will enable them to learn to write programs. This skill will not need to be acquired by everyone. Just as almost everyone has an automobile but few know how to fix the engine or make other repairs, few students and teachers will need to learn to write programs for the computer. However, every child and teacher should have the opportunity to learn to control the cmputer and to make it work for them by using appropriate software.

The Problems

What are the difficulties in getting us from where we are to where we could be? The greatest problem is that educational systems are very slow to change. Innovation in education is slow to come and sometimes never does. To realize the full potential of microcomputer use in schools, we must restructure the way we visualize the educational process. We must be willing to let a machine (the microcomputer) do some of the teaching job so that teachers will be free to work more directly in guiding the educational process for individual students.

Teachers must be trained in the use of microcomputers. This training will take time because institutions of higher education will have to retrain the teachers who are already in the schools and also provide appropriate microcomputer learning experiences for those students who are preparing to become teachers. Also, institutions of higher education must acquire the necessary equipment and personnel for training.

The greatest constraint is probably the money needed to institute the type of program which will provide an effective education using microcomputers. Most schools that currently have microcomputers have gotten them through the efforts of parents' groups. Often the lower socioeconomic level schools do not have computers because parents are often less active in the educational process and fewer funds are available. Thus, the individual school districts are going to have to be willing to appropriate the necessary funds so that all schools will have sufficient computers to reach all of the children.

Microcomputers certainly have the capacity for revolutionizing the educational process. This revolution and ultimate improvement in our schools will happen only when 1) we are willing to make innovative changes in our teaching; 2) we train our teachers to use the microcomputer as a tool to improve the educational process; 3) we invest the necessary funds to acquire a sufficient number of computers for them to be educationally beneficial; 4) instructionally effective software is available at reasonable prices; and 5) state education agencies, school districts, individual schools and teachers have coordinated plans for how the microcomputer will be used.

THE IMPORTANCE OF RECOGNIZING A CHILD'S LEARNING STYLE

At the opening of school many students are excited and enthusiastic. They have made comments since the beginning of August such as, "I can't wait for school to start, I wonder who my new teacher will be, I hope I will need new school supplies." These are the students that teachers delight in welcoming the first day of school and describe as their best and most enjoyable students. There is, however, a second group of students; those who become upset at the mention of vacation ending; those who are not able to pull themselves out of bed the first day of school but have been up by 6:00 AM every day of the summer. This is the group of students that teachers find most challenging. They pose particular problems for parents because when all other strategies fail, the teacher may look for sources of blame and eventually place that blame on the parent. There are several reasons that this group of reluctant learners may exist, and one reason is that the student's learning style does not match the teacher's teaching style.

Learning styles and teaching styles are areas in which there are many current research studies and recommendations. These, unfortunately, are often not known or utilized by teachers and parents.

Research in neuroscience and particularly neuropsychology has revealed that there are two types of learners. Those who learn verbally and those who learn spatially. In other words, there are those who learn best by talking, listening, and reading; and others who learn best from seeing and touching. The dominant hemisphere of the brain determines the style of learning and luckily most students are verbal learners. As can be easily guessed, the student who learns best through the verbal mode is going to be the most successful in school because by nature, schools are very verbal places with lots of board work, seat work, and class discussions. The visual/spatial learner who learns best from seeing and perhaps even feeling the completed activity and then completing the activity him or herself is at a disadvantage in a verbally oriented classroom.

There are other components of learning style. Many students have a dominant modality: visual, auditory, or kinesthetic and learn best when information is presented using that modality. Some learners perfer to use all modalities and learn best when instruction uses amultisensory approach. Additional components of learning style include time of day, structure, size of group, reinforcement, setting, noise level and motivation.

When a teacher and parent are faced with a reluctant learner, one of the first interventions is to determine how the student learns best. Of course the question is, "How do I do this?" The best strategy is to watch the student learn a new task that s/he wants to learn and analyze how the student learned the task. Another strategy is to ask the student how s/he learned the task.

Once the parent, teacher, and student have identified the student's learning style, instruction should incorporate teaching strategies which consider the learning style. Best learning occurs when teaching style matches learning style.

Perhaps some reluctant learners will become less so if their particular learning style is considered more in the educational environment.

THE BIFUNCTIONAL BRAIN
IN THE CLASSROOM

As researchers discover more about the human brain and how it functions, the findings are being translated into useful information for parents and teachers. This information can be used to help children expand their awareness and use their intellectual potential in ways that have not been traditionally emphasized.

It is now thought that the human brain is bifunctional. This means that the left half and right half of the brain have fairly specific tasks. They learn things in different ways and solve problems in unique ways.

For the majority of people, the left half of the brain is responsible for processing language. It analyzes experiences and relates the present to the past. It is very logical, orderly and sequential. It deals with facts and is responsible for building new constructs.

For the majority of people, the right half of the brain is the creative half. It thinks in images, detects patterns, and responds to novelty and the unknown. It is innovative and visionary and much more performance oriented than the left half of the brain. This imaginative, intuitive half of the brain is also more emotional.

Most of what happens in our classrooms emphasizes the use of the left half of the brain. The emphasis on the use of written and spoken language to learn and give evidence of learning makes this obvious. At the same time, the creative, intuitive, more emotional right brain is left to atrophy. By doing this we are ignoring a great deal of our intellectual potential.

Parents and teachers are the people who must use their own creative abilities to reverse this trend. For example, rather than ask questions that have one correct answer, ask questions that have many possible answers, and accept all of them. Also, when children use their intuition to solve problems, allow them to do so. We tend to dismiss any use of intuitive knowing as unscientific and therefore unacceptable. As another example, use visualization or imaging by having children close their eyes and picture whatever they are learning. This uses the right brain to reinforce their learning.

There are many books available in local bookstores that are written about this and related subjects. For parents and teachers who are interested in learning more about this subject, we would suggest that they allow their intuitive brains to help them choose one.

A PRODUCTIVE SUMMER VACATION

The summer is a period of time when children can lose many of the academic and social skills that they have acquired during the school year. This loss is particularly possible for children who require much repetition and review in order to learn. Children, like adults, need some rest and relaxation, and planning demanding activities for the entire summer can be detrimental. However, parents and teachers can plan so that children will experience an enriching and productive, yet relaxing and enjoyable summer.

What inexpensive but worthwhile activities are available? The possibilities are limitless when parents, teachers, and children put their imagination, creativity, and resourcefulness to use.

When planning summer activities for children, parents and teachers should obtain input from children. In fact, one very useful and practical activity for parents and children in late May or early June is to make a summer calendar. Before making the calendar, the child should make a list of things that she or he would like to do. The parent should guide the child in making this list and help the child decide on realistic and valuable activities.

Many excellent community activities are available. Some of these are free and others have a minimal charge. Libraries usually have very good summer programs, many organizations sponsor summer enrichment series, and many community sponsored sports activities as well as church related camps and events are available.

Parents and teachers should caution children not to restrict themselves to group or community sponsored activities. Instruction and activities at home can be very enjoyable. Children may be interested in learning to cook, garden, paint, write, or play new games. Parents can assist their children by providing the necessary encouragement and resources to engage in these activities.

One restriction that parents should make for their children is the amount of time to be spent viewing television. During the summer it is quite easy to get into the habit of watching so much television that opportunities for using time in more beneficial and educational activities is lost. Turn off the television and read, talk, or play together instead. The easiest way to get started on this project is for the family members to choose a half hour that they would normally have the television on, and then choose an activity to take its place. Even if everyone just walks around the block together, the interaction and communication could do wonders for the whole family.

How can teachers help parents and children plan for summer? Teachers can recommend age-appropriate activities. This list can include academic enrichment as well as remedial suggestions. Teachers could provide a reading list, math activities and games, writing exercises, etc. These recommendations should not appear to be drudgery, but fun and exciting.

Planning and organization help ensure that activities will be productive and worthwhile. By helping children plan their summers, parents and teachers are teaching valuable planning and organizational skills as well as ensuring that a three month period of time will not be wasted.

INDEX

A

Acceleration, 91
Attention deficit disorder, 86-88

B

Behavior modification, 27-28, 87
Bifunctional brain, 94, 104

C

Communication
  with children, 22-24, 83-84
  with parents, 5-7, 9, 69-70
Computers, 93, 99-101
Consequences, 25-26
Consistency, 57
Contracting, 34, 66
Cooperation, 5, 8-9, 11
Corporal punishment, 45-50
Criticism trap, 51-53
Curriculum, hidden, 72

D

Discipline
  consistency, 57
  contingency contracting, 34
  corporal punishment, 45-50
  home-school contracts, 35-38
  response cost, 41, 49
  rewards, 31-33, 38
  "SPI" approach, 29-30
  time-out, 43, 49
  token economies, 38, 40
Discipline quotient, 54, 58, 60-61

E

Enrichment, 91
Expectations, 21-21, 56

G

Gifted and talented, 91-92
Grading, 63, 68
Guidance counselor, 78

H

Homework, 63, 65-67
Hyperactivity, 86, 95
Hypoactivity, 95

L

Labeling, 77
Learning disabilities, 85
Learning style, 93, 102-103

M

Modeling, 58-59, 72

N

Nutrition, 93, 95

P

Parent-teacher conferences, 1, 6, 12-13
Parent-teacher organization, 17
Peer tutors, 71
Problem-solving conferences, 14-15
Punishment, 41, 43, 51, 56-57

R

Reinforcement, 43-44
Reinforcers, 31, 46, 52
Resource rooms, 76
Response cost, 41
Rewards, 31

S

School phobia, 89-90
School psychologist, 78

School routine, 63
Self-concept, 8-9, 22
Self-contained classroom, 76-77
Special education, 75-76, 85-86, 91
Special personnel, 78-80
 remedial teachers, 79
 resource teachers, 79
 school psychologist, 78
 speech therapist, 79
"SPI Approach, 29-30
Stress, 81-83
Support system, 17
Systematic desensitatization, 89

T

Teachable moments, 73-74
Teacher morale, 1, 16-19
Time management, 93, 97-98
Time-out, 43
Token economies, 38
Tracking, 91
Tutoring, 71

V

Vacation, summer, 94, 106-107
Volunteers, 63-64, 69-70